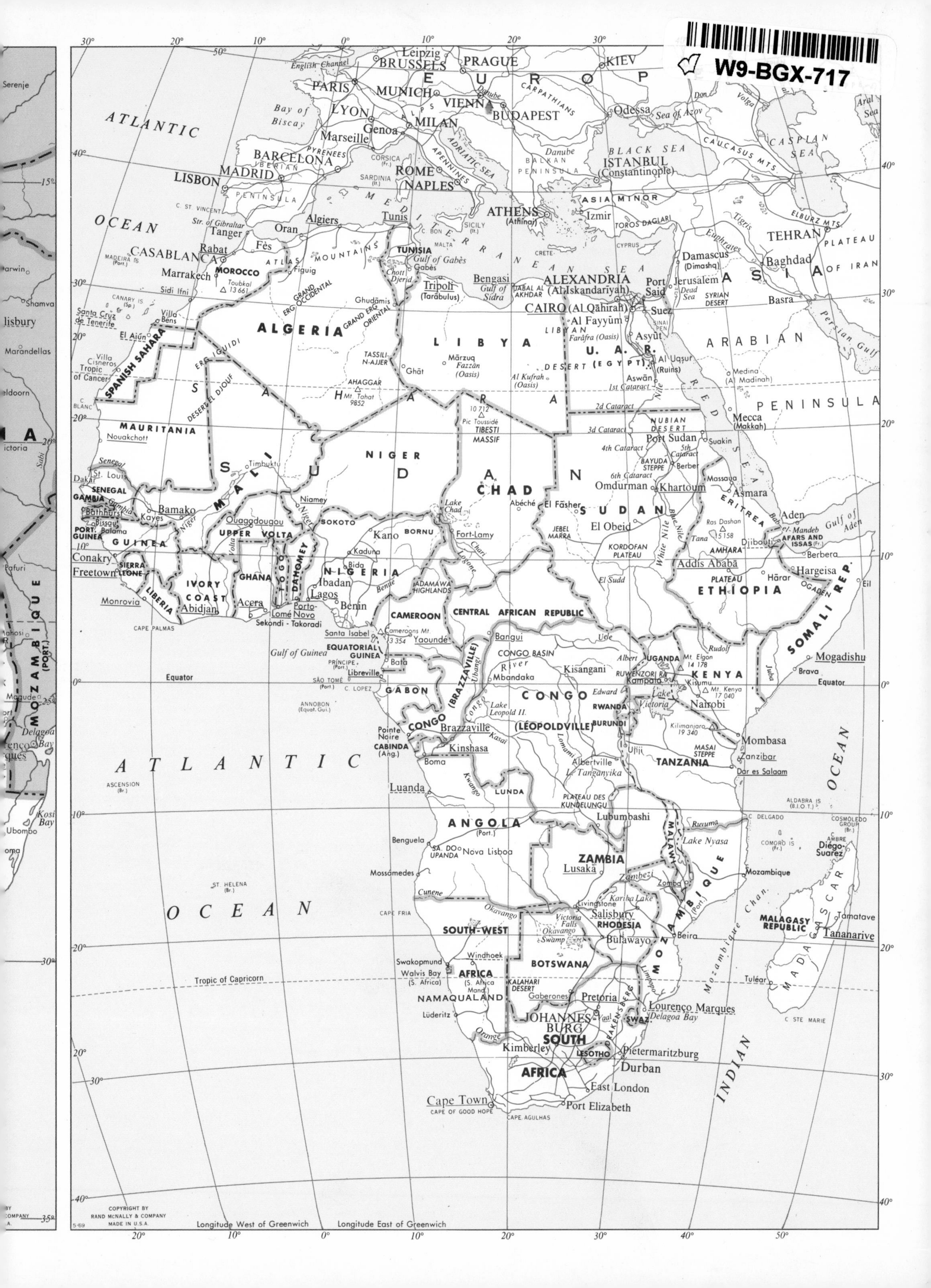

EUROPE
Leipzig
BRUSSELS
PRAGUE
KIEV
English Channel
PARIS
MUNICH
Danube
CARPATHIANS
VIENNA
BUDAPEST
Odessa
Sea of Azov
Don
Volga
Aral Sea
Bay of Biscay
LYON
ALPS
MILAN
Genoa
Marseille
ATLANTIC
PYRENEES
IBERIAN PENINSULA
BARCELONA
MADRID
LISBON
CORSICA (Fr.)
SARDINIA (It.)
ROME
NAPLES
ADRIATIC SEA
APENNINES
BALKAN PENINSULA
BLACK SEA
ISTANBUL (Constantinople)
CAUCASUS MTS.
CASPIAN SEA
C. ST. VINCENT
Str. of Gibraltar
Tanger
Oran
Algiers
Tunis
MEDITERRANEAN SEA
SICILY (It.)
ATHENS (Athínai)
ASIA MINOR
Izmir
TOROS DAGLARI
ELBURZ MTS.
Tigris
Euphrates
TEHRAN
PLATEAU OF IRAN
OCEAN
C. BON
MALTA
CRETE
CYPRUS
CASABLANCA
Rabat
Fès
MOROCCO
ATLAS MOUNTAINS
TUNISIA
Gulf of Gabès
Gabès
Figuig
Chott Djerid
Damascus (Dimashq)
Baghdad
ASIA
MADEIRA IS. (Port.)
Marrakech
Toubkal 13 661
Tripoli (Tarābulus)
Bengasi
Gulf of Sidra
JABAL AL AKHDAR
ALEXANDRIA (Al Iskandarīyah)
Port Said
Jerusalem
Dead Sea
SYRIAN DESERT
Basra
Sidi Ifni
CANARY IS. (Sp.)
Santa Cruz de Tenerife
Villa Bens
GRAND ERG OCCIDENTAL
Ghudāmis
GRAND ERG ORIENTAL
CAIRO (Al Qāhirah)
Suez
Al Fayyūm
SINAI PEN.
Persian Gulf
ALGERIA
El Aiún
LIBYA
LIBYAN DESERT
Farāfra (Oasis)
Asyūt
U. A. R. (EGYPT)
Al Uqsur (Ruins)
ARABIAN PENINSULA
SPANISH SAHARA
Villa Cisneros
Tropic of Cancer
ERG IGUIDI
DESERT EL DJOUF
TASSILI-N-AJJER
Ghāt
Mārzuq
Fazzān (Oasis)
Al Kufrah (Oasis)
Aswān
Nile
Medina (Al Madīnah)
RED SEA
1st Cataract
SAHARA
AHAGGAR
Mt. Tahat 9852
C. BLANC
10 712
Pic Toussidé
TIBESTI MASSIF
2d Cataract
Mecca (Makkah)
MAURITANIA
Nouakchott
NUBIAN DESERT
3d Cataract
Port Sudan
Suakin
Senegal
St. Louis
Timbuktu
NIGER
SUDAN
4th Cataract
5th Cataract
BAYUDA STEPPE
Berber
Dakar
SENEGAL
GAMBIA
Gambia
Bathurst
MALI
CHAD
Abéché
6th Cataract
Omdurman
Khartoum
Massaua
Asmara
ERITREA
Bamako
Kayes
Niamey
Niger
El Fāsher
SUDAN
El Obeid
Blue Nile
White Nile
Ras Dashan 15 158
Aden
Bab el-Mandeb
Gulf of Aden
Bissau
PORT. GUINEA
Bolama
GUINEA
Ouagadougou
UPPER VOLTA
SOKOTO
Kano
BORNU
Lake Chad
Fort-Lamy
Chari
JEBEL MARRA
KORDOFAN PLATEAU
Tana
Djibouti
AFARS AND ISSAS (Fr.)
AMHARA
Berbera
Conakry
Freetown
SIERRA LEONE
Volta
GHANA
TOGO
DAHOMEY
Kaduna
Bida
NIGERIA
Logone
Addis Ababa
Hargeisa
Hārar
Eil
IVORY COAST
Abidjan
Accra
Lomé
Porto-Novo
Ibadan
Lagos
Benin
Benue
ADAMAWA HIGHLANDS
El Sudd
PLATEAU
ETHIOPIA
OGADEN
SOMALI REP.
Monrovia
LIBERIA
CAPE PALMAS
Sekondi - Takoradi
CAMEROON
CENTRAL AFRICAN REPUBLIC
Santa Isabel
Cameroons Mt. 13 354
Yaoundé
Bangui
Uele
Rudolf
Gulf of Guinea
EQUATORIAL GUINEA
PRINCIPE (Port.)
Bata
CONGO BASIN
Ubangi
River
Albert
UGANDA
Mt. Elgon 14 178
KENYA
Juba
Mogadishu
Equator
Libreville
SÃO TOMÉ (Port.)
C. LOPEZ
GABON
Mbandaka
Kisangani
RUWENZORI RA.
Kampala
Kisumu
Brava
Mt. Kenya 17 040
Edward
Lake Victoria
Nairobi
ANNOBON (Equat. Gui.)
CONGO (BRAZZAVILLE)
Lake Leopold II.
CONGO (LÉOPOLDVILLE)
RWANDA
BURUNDI
Pointe Noire
Brazzaville
Kasai
Lomami
Kilimanjaro 19 340
MASAI STEPPE
Mombasa
CABINDA (Ang.)
Kinshasa
Boma
Ujiji
TANZANIA
Zanzibar
Dar es Salaam
ATLANTIC
Albertville
L. Tanganyika
ASCENSION (Br.)
Luanda
Kwango
LUNDA
PLATEAU DES KUNDELUNGU
ALDABRA IS. (B.I.O.T.)
Lubumbashi
C. DELGADO
COSMOLEDO GROUP (Br.)
ANGOLA (Port.)
MALAWI
Ruvuma
Lake Nyasa
Benguela
SA. DO UPANDA
Nova Lisboa
COMORO IS. (Fr.)
AMBRE
Diégo-Suarez
ZAMBIA
Lusaka
Mossâmedes
Zambezi
Zomba
MOZAMBIQUE (Port.)
Mozambique
ST. HELENA (Br.)
Cunene
Livingstone
Kariba Lake
OCEAN
CAPE FRIA
Okavango
Victoria Falls
Salisbury
RHODESIA
Mozambique Chan.
MADAGASCAR
Tamatave
SOUTH-WEST AFRICA
Okavango Swamp
Bulawayo
Beira
MALAGASY REPUBLIC
Tananarive
Windhoek
BOTSWANA
Swakopmund
Walvis Bay (S. Africa)
(S. Africa Mand.)
Tropic of Capricorn
Limpopo
KALAHARI DESERT
Tuléar
NAMAQUALAND
Gaberones
Pretoria
Lüderitz
JOHANNESBURG
Vaal
DRAKENSBERG
Lourenço Marques
Delagoa Bay
SWAZ.
C. STE MARIE
Orange
SOUTH AFRICA
Kimberley
LESOTHO
Pietermaritzburg
Durban
INDIAN OCEAN
East London
Cape Town
CAPE OF GOOD HOPE
CAPE AGULHAS
Port Elizabeth
Longitude West of Greenwich
Longitude East of Greenwich
Serenje
Darwin
Shamva
Salisbury
Marandellas
Eldoorn
Victoria
Sabi
Pafuri
MOZAMBIQUE (PORT.)
Maqude
Delagoa Bay
Kosi Bay
Ubombo
5-69

LIFE WORLD LIBRARY

SOUTH AFRICA

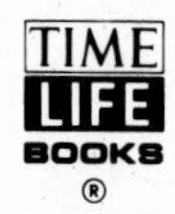

LIFE WORLD LIBRARY
LIFE NATURE LIBRARY
TIME READING PROGRAM
THE LIFE HISTORY OF THE UNITED STATES
LIFE SCIENCE LIBRARY
INTERNATIONAL BOOK SOCIETY
GREAT AGES OF MAN
TIME-LIFE LIBRARY OF ART
TIME-LIFE LIBRARY OF AMERICA
FOODS OF THE WORLD
THIS FABULOUS CENTURY

LIFE WORLD LIBRARY

SOUTH AFRICA

by Tom Hopkinson

and the Editors of

TIME-LIFE BOOKS

TIME-LIFE BOOKS NEW YORK

COVER: A Xhosa woman and her
child, residents of the Transkei
in southeastern South Africa,
peer out of their whitewashed,
thatch-roofed hut beneath
the lush, green mountains of
the Drakensberg range.

ABOUT THE WRITER

Tom Hopkinson, who wrote the interpretive chapters for this volume of the LIFE World Library, worked as a journalist in London for nearly 30 years before leaving his native England to live in Africa. He was the editor of *Picture Post* from 1940 to 1950, and also edited the small, lively magazine called *Lilliput* at the same time. He later served as features editor of the *News-Chronicle*. In 1958 Mr. Hopkinson went to South Africa, where for three and a half years he edited *Drum,* a magazine produced largely for, and by, Africans. He traveled repeatedly to Ghana and Nigeria organizing the local editions of *Drum,* and was in the Congo during the fighting which followed Congolese independence. During the winter of 1968-1969 he was a visiting professor in the School of Journalism at the University of Minnesota. Mr. Hopkinson, who is married, is at present Senior Fellow in Press Studies at the University of Sussex, Brighton, England. He has written a number of books, including two collections of short stories and a short critical appraisal of the late George Orwell. His most recent book, *In the Fiery Continent,* which was published in the United States in 1963, tells of his experiences in Africa while editing *Drum.*

Published simultaneously in Canada.
Library of Congress catalogue card number 64-23718.
School and library distribution by Silver Burdett Company, Morristown, New Jersey.

Contents

TIME-LIFE BOOKS

EDITOR
Maitland A. Edey
EXECUTIVE EDITOR
Jerry Korn
TEXT DIRECTOR Martin Mann
ART DIRECTOR Sheldon Cotler
CHIEF OF RESEARCH
Beatrice T. Dobie
PICTURE EDITOR
Robert G. Mason
Assistant Text Directors:
Harold C. Field, Ogden Tanner
Assistant Art Director: Arnold C. Holeywell
Assistant Chief of Research: Martha T. Goolrick

•

PUBLISHER
Rhett Austell
Associate Publisher: Walter C. Rohrer
Assistant Publisher: Carter Smith
General Manager: Joseph C. Hazen Jr.
Business Manager: John D. McSweeney
Production Manager: Louis Bronzo

•

Sales Director: Joan D. Manley
Promotion Director: Beatrice K. Tolleris
Managing Director, International: John A. Millington

LIFE WORLD LIBRARY

SERIES EDITOR: Oliver E. Allen
Editorial Staff for *South Africa:*
Assistant Editor: David S. Thomson
Designer: Ben Schultz
Chief Researcher: Grace Brynolson
Researchers: Paula von Haimberger Arno, Jill Adams,
June Omura Goldberg, Rebecca Chaitin

EDITORIAL PRODUCTION
Color Director: Robert L. Young
Assistant: James J. Cox
Copy Staff: Rosalind Stubenberg, Helen Isaacs, Florence Keith
Picture Department: Dolores A. Littles, Barbara Sullivan
Traffic: Arthur A. Goldberger
Art Assistants: James D. Smith, John M. Woods

The interpretive text for the chapters of this book was written by Tom Hopkinson and the picture essays were written by Edmund V. White and David S. Thomson. Many of the photographs were taken by Grey Villet. Valuable assistance was provided by the following individuals and departments of Time Inc.: Editorial Production, Robert W. Boyd Jr.; Editorial Reference, Peter Draz; Picture Collection, Doris O'Neil; Photographic Laboratory, George Karas; TIME-LIFE News Service, Murray J. Gart; Reprints Editor, Stanley Fillmore.

Introduction

Everybody wants to know about South Africa. It is always in the headlines and throbs in the world's conscience like a blister on the heel of the African continent.

It is a country ruled by an oligarchy whose forefathers came from Europe. It is the only nation in the world where there is a sizable minority of white people in a country predominantly black, and the whites in fact constitute almost one fifth of the total population of 17 million people.

South Africa has been settled for more than 300 years and is only 30 or 40 years younger than the United States of America. Unfortunately, its development has been bedeviled by racial tensions and hostility. Many of its mineral and agricultural resources are unexploited, perhaps in part because it seeks to solve its racial problems by its policy of "apartheid," of complete and ever-stricter segregation.

When the rest of the world complains of this reactionary solution, South Africa is quick to point out that the United States avoided its original racial problem by exterminating the indigenous people of America, and that in any event America's present racial problems have little in common with those of South Africa. The Negroes are a minority group in the U.S.A.; but it is the whites who form the minority group in South Africa and who, providentially in their own estimation, still hold the upper hand.

South Africa is a land of perplexing contrasts. Its racial policies are abhorrent to the rest of the world, though the world recognizes that they are prompted by a fear of absorption. It is the only country which is trying to put the clock back, and is apparently willing to do so however much it hurts. Yet at the same time its economy is booming. It has never been more prosperous. Its gold and diamond mining production is immense. Foreign financiers fall over one another to invest in South African enterprises; and foreign industries, producing everything from motorcars to textiles, set up factory after factory on South African soil.

How can these things be? How can this country be so economically successful and at the same time pursue a racial course that shames and horrifies the world outside it?

Anyone who wishes to be at all intelligently informed about South Africa must know something about its geography, its history, its development, its hopes and its fears. No better guide could be found than Tom Hopkinson, whose firsthand knowledge of South Africa is evident on every page of this book.

The question that should be exercising the minds of South Africans today is: In this prosperous land, how can a truly multiracial society be established in which whites, Coloreds (mixed groups), blacks, Indians, Malays and Chinese can all play a responsible part? The question is surely one of the most demanding in the world today, and it would be exciting to be able to try and work it out in terms of justice, toleration and good will. South Africa, at the time of writing, is far from reaching the point at which this can be done. Its present policies are anti-Christian, inhuman and, let it be added, suicidal. It has deliberately thrown away chance after chance. Those who love that country of immense potential pray that it may come to its senses while there is still time.

RT. REV. JOOST DE BLANK
former Archbishop of Cape Town
and Metropolitan of the Anglican Church
in South Africa

DOING BEADWORK, a woman of the Shangaan tribe embroiders a basket while her children play nearby. Although she has a modern home *(background)* in a housing development for Africans outside Johannesburg, she wears tribal dress.

1

The Favored Tip of a Continent

IT is difficult to imagine anywhere in the world a country more blessed by nature than South Africa. From the Atlantic to the Indian Ocean, from the Cape to the borders of Rhodesia, it displays an amazing variety of natural beauties and attractions. Moreover, they are still largely unspoiled.

Until less than a century ago South Africa was cut off from the flow of modern development, so that the country was spared the worst ravages suffered by more advanced nations in the early Industrial Revolution. Learning from the mistakes of others, the South Africans have not destroyed their landscape but instead have provided—through roads, railroads and airports—the means to travel easily about it and enjoy it. The cities and towns as a rule belong in the countryside; they concentrate its character and interest; they have not devoured it and laid it waste.

Among South Africa's natural wonders are tremendous mountains; glorious beaches, including a stretch of year-round holiday coastline 300 miles long; upland plains still roamed by wild animals in herds and droves; and deserts which, when the spring rains fall, unfold overnight into flower gardens. Although rainfall is insufficient in South Africa, and more than half of the country is barren, the farmer's loss is the visitor's gain, and the climate over much of the country adds a new dimension to life—one can make plans with the certainty of having sunshine. The soil, though thin in general, is in Natal so rich that people living there say: "Throw seeds into the garden when you go to bed, and you won't be able to see out of your window in the morning." In the eastern Transvaal there are farms on the face of the escarpment where, over quite a small acreage of ground, every known variety of fruit is grown. On top of the escarpment grow the pears and apples of cool climates. Farther down are the peaches, oranges, lemons and figs of semitropical countries. In the rich, warm hollows several thousand feet below grow tropical fruits such as pineapples, bananas, mangoes and papaws. With so favorable a climate and so wide a variety of physical conditions, South Africa is a land ideally suited for sport—sailing, swimming, surfing, skin diving, big-game fishing, mountaineering, horseback riding, hunting and every other kind of recreation.

And all this with a road system along which one can drive—if one's car allows—75 miles in the first hour, 150 in two hours or 300 in four hours. Many drivers make a point of covering the 900-odd miles from Cape Town to Johannesburg in 15 or 16 hours, with no stop for a night's rest. Internal air travel is easy and convenient, and South Africa is the only country on the African continent with a complete network of railroads.

WITH its highly efficient public services, its outward covering of public order, its wide range of sports and amusements, its luxurious homes and holiday resorts, and with the ease of a life where attentive service can be cheaply bought, South Africa makes an overwhelming impression on most casual visitors. It seems a piece of the white world set down, under peculiarly happy conditions of climate and surroundings, in what is usually considered a dark and backward continent.

Furthermore, South Africa does not, like so many countries, suffer from overcrowding. For a territory which is more than twice the size of France, or bigger than Texas, Oklahoma and New Mexico combined, a population of 19 million is not large; but for those who find humanity's differences a source of interest rather than resentment, it is fascinatingly varied. If a man from Mars wished to see in a single afternoon the full range the human race can offer, he could not do better than walk through Cape Town's streets. In South Africa as a whole he could find every variety of man, and life at every level. He could experience existence at the prehistoric level of the Bushman, live tribally in the Reserves, recover an early-19th Century manner of life on remote farms in the Cape valleys, hear the pulse of urbanized Africa in the black townships near the gold mines and finally, in the white suburbs of Johannesburg or Pretoria, find a luxury unrivaled, perhaps, anywhere except in California or Rio de Janeiro.

THOUGH its landscape is enormously varied, the physical formation of South Africa can be simply described. It consists of a lofty plateau, rising to peaks more than 11,000 feet high, surrounded by a steep escarpment. The west coast is barren and largely desert. The only considerable river is the Orange, far to the north, which serves as a boundary between South Africa and South-West Africa. The east coast is much more beautiful and fertile, but here the rivers plunge headlong through the escarpment to the warm waters of the Indian Ocean, building up in most cases a sand bar across their own mouths, so that few are navigable at all and none for any distance.

From Cape Town northward up the west coast to the border of South-West Africa there are no harbors except for a few small fishing ports. There are none along the south coast either, until one comes to Port Elizabeth, 500 miles to the east of Cape Town. Along the whole eastern coast there are only two ports, East London and Durban. No doubt it was this shortage of harbors, together with the grim nature of the west coast and the forbidding inland barrier of the escarpment—up and down whose boulder-strewn slopes the pioneers' ox wagons had to be hauled piece by piece—which prevented the country from being opened up earlier than it was. The loftiness of the inland plateau, however, is a blessing, since it is this which gives the interior its agreeable climate—a moderate heat relieved by rainstorms and thunder showers in summer, and a winter of cloudless days reaching a pleasant warmth at midday, but with nights that are always cool and fresh.

Looking at the interior of South Africa first, the key word is "veld," meaning a grassy plain. The

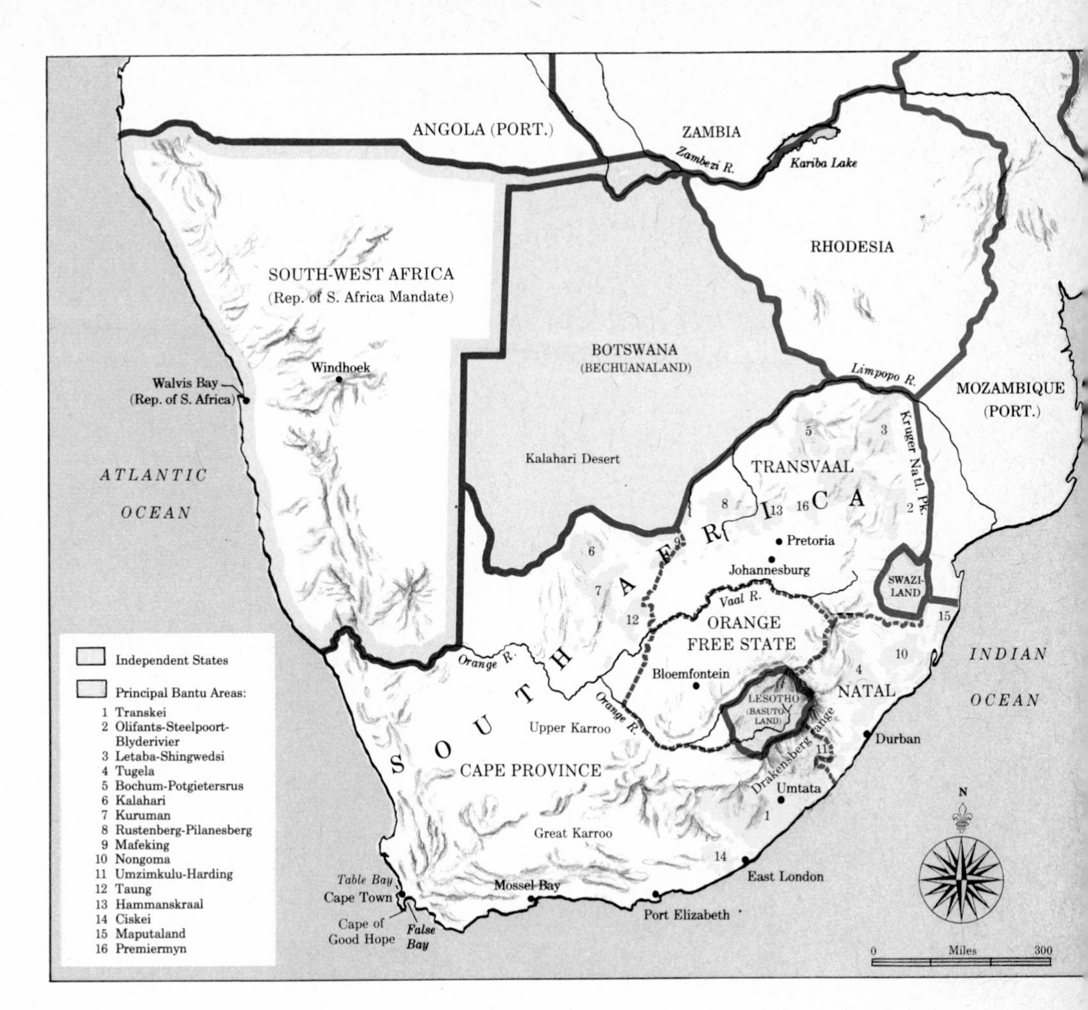

MAJOR AREAS of southern Africa are shown at right. The Republic of South Africa *(bottom),* which is the subject of this volume, comprises four provinces: Cape Province, Orange Free State, Transvaal and Natal. The Bantu areas numbered 1 to 16 are shown as they were in 1956; they are currently being consolidated, so as eventually to form seven or eight tribal "homelands" organized by the Government for administrative purposes. Botswana, Lesotho and Swaziland, formerly controlled by Great Britain, are now politically independent, but are economically dependent on South Africa. South-West Africa, under German control from 1883 to 1915, was given the status of a League of Nations mandate territory after World War I and awarded to South Africa to administer. After World War II, the United Nations took over responsibility for many former League mandates, but South Africa, considering South-West Africa an integral part of its domain, has defied the U.N. and all but incorporated the territory. The South-West African port of Walvis Bay is an outright possession of South Africa.

highveld and the middleveld, like an enormous prairie, cover most of the Transvaal and the Orange Free State, two of South Africa's four provinces, and then continue on northward for hundreds of miles across the Rhodesias into Tanganyika and Kenya. In the northern and eastern sections of the Transvaal spreads the bushveld, dry, flat country covered with scrub. Farther eastward over the escarpment lie the well-watered foothills and fertile valleys known as the lowveld. Here nature closes in, and in place of the highveld, with its low horizon and soaring cloud patterns, one finds oneself in deep canyons with waterfalls and in shady patches of forest. The lowveld includes the 8,000 square miles of the Kruger National Park, that cherished patch of early Africa, teeming with animal and bird life, which is South Africa's biggest tourist attraction.

Smallest of the four South African provinces is Natal, which stretches along the Indian Ocean from the Umzimkulu River to the southern border of the Portuguese controlled territory of Mozambique. On the west, Natal touches the two newly independent states of Lesotho and Swaziland, and on the south, the area known as the Transkei, first of the partially self-governing territories for Africans known as Bantustans.

Natal is a fertile land of grassy hills and valleys, subtropical beaches, far-ranging plains and uplands. In a huge arc straddling the Lesotho border stand the towering heights of the Drakensberg, among them 9,856-foot-high Cathedral Peak, Giant's Castle (10,878 feet) and Champagne Castle (11,081 feet). The long seaboard includes two wonderful stretches of holiday coastline: the south coast, running down from Durban to link up with the Transkei's Wild Coast, and the north coast, which fringes Zululand and is broken up into estuaries and lagoons in which swarm crocodiles; part of this region, however, is now a testing ground for South Africa's missile program.

has a subtropical climate—extremely hot on the seacoast in summer and agreeably warm in winter. It is one of the main centers of the English-speaking people and contains four fifths of all the Indians in the Republic of South Africa.

The Cape Province is the oldest, and also the most varied, of the four. The southwestern Cape, near Cape Town itself, is a country of rich valleys and rugged mountain ranges, running down to a broken coastline with many bays and beaches. North of Cape Town, the west coast region known as Namaqualand is barren and largely desert. Only in the spring, when the year's meager allowance of rain falls, does the desolate landscape burst into bloom and the arid expanse is carpeted with wildflowers.

The southeastern part of the province is again a land of rolling hills and mountain ranges, through which runs the highway known as the Garden Route, leading to the two big ports of East London and Port Elizabeth. Inland the most unusual feature is the semidesert known as the Great Karroo, a moon landscape of scrub-covered veld out of which rise flat-topped hills, or *koppies,* whose summits seem to have been sliced off with a knife. Here too, a good fall of rain brings a sudden outburst of wildflowers from what appeared to be nothing but stones and sand. In all, the Cape Province can show 2,600 species of indigenous wildflowers, the largest concentration in the world.

South Africa is not only a land of haunting beauty. In its variety of landscape and climate there seems to be something which appeals to people of the most different natures, origins and backgrounds. "In a crowded London street," says one white South African who lives in exile in England, "I will see a colored handkerchief wrapped round a head, or smell a pile of oranges on a barrow, and my blood will bound. [I . . . and others in exile . . .] know how the bushes clamber down to the beach, how the pine trees gather in the dusk, how the bleached earth cracks in the Karroo beneath the hot, flat sky. South Africa remains our country, whatever passports we carry, and wherever we live, we remain—grudgingly or gladly, always helplessly—with its people. . . ."

These sentences form almost the last words of *Into Exile* by Ronald Segal, who left South Africa after the infamous Sharpeville massacre of 1960, in which 70 Africans were shot down by the police in a moment of blind panic. The sentences come as a sudden outburst of feeling in a book full of argument and exposition. The same feelings are expressed in many different ways by many different people.

"But this fierce country is exciting too," writes the famous South African author Alan Paton. "Would I live somewhere else? Sometimes I would, but not now. For she evokes something deep and powerful, that satisfies even when it is painful, something exciting and depressing, attracting and repelling."

A MIXED POPULATION

Four main groups make up South Africa's population (1967 estimate: 18,733,000). More than 80 per cent was made up of nonwhite, including Coloreds (people of mixed ancestry) and Asians.

GROUP	NUMBER	PERCENT
Africans	12,750,000	68.20
Whites	3,563,000	19.03
Coloreds	1,859,000	9.77
Asians	561,000	3.00

In Ghana not long ago, a journalist from South Africa arrived at the Ambassador Hotel in Accra where half a dozen African political exiles—members of the banned African National Congress and Pan-African Congress—were living. They were staying in comfort, free to order anything they wanted. The journalist had last seen them dodging about Johannesburg, fearing arrest daily and not knowing where or how they would next eat, glancing along every street before they ventured down it. But in a moment they were crowding around the newcomer.

"Gosh! Were you in Jo'burg this morning? What was it like, man? Is it still the same?" And after a dozen enquiries after their friends, one added: "It isn't the same here, man. We don't feel properly alive. Look at the trees!" He threw his hand up toward the palms. "They're not real trees like we have at home, man. . . . I sometimes wish one of these cops would turn round and chase after us. Give us the feeling we were home again."

The tragedy of South Africa is not that those who are living in the country hate it. Quite the contrary. The outside world may hate South Africa; those who belong to the country love it. The tragedy is that their devotion—unless it is along the narrow lines ordered by the Government—is not required and is actually repelled. "We can't even fight for our country," an ardent African politician exclaimed angrily over a drink. "Negroes can fight for the United States. They may not feel satisfied with their situation—but at least they could fight for their country in a war. We're shut out from that as well. They wouldn't even let us die—voluntarily, I mean."

The position then is that an enormous amount of patriotism and devotion is given to South Africa by the approximately 19 million people living there. But these millions are so split and divided—by race, color, religion, culture, background and in every other way—that the South Africas they wish to build are totally different countries, having almost nothing in common.

WHY do the different groups in South Africa want different things? Why can there be no agreement—as elsewhere in the world—on a common policy and plan, or at least on some parts of a common policy which can be carried out now, while agreement is sought on the next stages? Why is it that four fifths of the population is kept permanently in subjection, without a vote or the hope of a vote through which they could influence and improve their condition? The answers to these questions are to be found partly in the history of South Africa, which we shall consider in the next chapters, but partly also in the racial composition of the country, which has no parallel anywhere else on earth.

By far the largest racial group in South Africa is that of the Africans. Made up of some hundreds of different tribes, speaking many languages and varying greatly in appearance, customs and level of cultural development, they are all officially classed as "Bantu" (a word which simply means "people"). In the late 1960s, according to an official estimate, there were about 13 million Africans, or Bantu, living in the Republic.

Of these millions, well over four million live something like their old tribal life in the Reserves. The Reserves occupy just under 13 per cent of the Republic, and have been tersely described as "vast rural slums whose chief export is their manpower." Most of the men from the Reserves are obliged to leave home to work in the mines or on European farms, since their own patches of ground will not supply a living for their families. Some five million Africans have come into the towns, where the men seek employment in mining, manufacture, transport and communications, or in personal service to Europeans. About three million more work—always for exceedingly low wages but not always under harsh conditions—on European farms.

THE second biggest group is that of the Europeans, or whites, which is over three million strong and constitutes the largest concentration of whites on the African continent. This group is split into two parts. Almost 60 per cent are Afrikaners, people mostly of Dutch and French descent having Afrikaans—an offshoot of Dutch—as their language. Just under 40 per cent have English as their native language, and for them no better names have yet been found than "English-speaking South Africans" or "the English-speaking section." In general terms, the Afrikaners dominate the country's political life through their Nationalist Party and largely control its agriculture, while the English-speaking section—which includes about 100,000 Jews—is strong in mining and industry and owns what are still the more widely read newspapers.

Though they work together in business or farming and cooperate in some aspects of public work, the two groups have not really merged. Differences of language, religion and culture have remained almost as sharp as they were at the passing in 1909 of the Act of Union, which, it was hoped, would lead to a steady coalescing of the two peoples. Even of social contact there is astonishingly little, and in recent years the Nationalist Government has deliberately put a stop—in the interest of keeping the Dutch-descended ruling group uncontaminated—to all attempts to bring the two peoples together through common schooling.

The third group is that known as the Coloreds. "Colored" in South Africa does not mean black but is applied to people of mixed descent. There are about two million of these people in South Africa, nine tenths of them living in Cape Province. This was the earliest province to be settled by whites, many of whom had brought no womenfolk with them. It includes Cape Town, which was for centuries a port of call for sailors, soldiers and travelers in passing vessels. Nationalist propagandists like to ascribe the million and a half Colored population to the activities of these visitors of passage; on the other hand, a Colored historian, Richard van der Ross, declares that the Colored people originated "nine months after the arrival of Jan van Riebeeck and his followers," the Dutchmen who founded the Cape settlement in 1652.

The Coloreds are not for the most part direct mixtures of black and white; they derive their origin from many strands: white settlers and farmers, Hottentot girls, Malay slaves imported by the Dutch during the 17th and 18th Centuries, women from Ceylon or from Madagascar. The result includes some of the most beautiful—and some of the most hideous—variations of the human face and form. Under Nationalist policy, Coloreds are rigidly excluded from the privileges of whites, with whom the Colored people feel that their real place lies and with whom they are anxious to associate. Light-skinned Coloreds frequently "try for white" or "play white," as it is called, just as light-skinned American Negroes sometimes choose to "pass." It is often a point of honor with a Colored family to accept the loss forever of a son or daughter who has crossed the line since, if they continue to associate, it is likely that the "play white" will be the subject of an official enquiry and be "downgraded."

Despite precautions and prejudice, it is estimated that in 300 years as many as a quarter of a million Coloreds may have passed into the white population, and that the odds are overwhelmingly against any white family which has lived in South Africa for 200 years being without some Colored blood.

THE final group is the so-called Indians, who could more correctly be described as Asians since not all of them have Indian origins. There are just over half a million of these Asians, four fifths of whom live in the province of Natal. There were virtually no Indians in South Africa before 1860, when the farmers of Natal began importing laborers from India to work in their sugar-cane fields. Indian immigration was stopped in 1911, but by then there was already a considerable population, which has increased proportionately more rapidly than the whites or Africans. It was formerly a Nationalist objective to repatriate all Indians, but the establishment in 1961 of a Department of Indian Affairs—though highly unpopular with the Indians—means that their permanent residence in South Africa has now been officially accepted. Being "nonwhite," they are not allowed to vote or to enjoy the educational and other facilities reserved for whites.

SUCH is the racial composition of South Africa. The Afrikaners accept persons of British origin as equals, but have so organized the country politically as to allow them little say in the conduct of affairs. They look upon Africans as inferiors who may remain in the Republic provided they work in menial occupations and are content to exercise no political rights outside the Reserves set aside for them. For the Coloreds, most Afrikaners feel sympathy, but this cannot, they explain, be translated into action, since to do so would be the "thin edge of the wedge" that might split the color bar.

Some extremist political leaders among the black Africans increasingly take the view—though the law does not allow them to express it—that the only people who have a right to live in South Africa are the Africans themselves and the Coloreds, whom they are willing to "adopt" as being politically homeless. However, the more moderate African leaders envision a "nonracial" society where all those who are willing to contribute to a peaceful South Africa will be accepted—a society that seems increasingly remote as the racial lines are more and more firmly drawn. It is perhaps significant that while the Afrikaner has always had a term of contempt (*Kafferboetie*, or Kaffir-lover) for the white who associates with blacks, the blacks have recently adopted their own term of abuse ("sell-out") for the black who associates with whites.

All in all, the population of South Africa is so compounded racially as to form a highly explosive mixture. The policies of the present-day Nationalist Party Government and the forces of change sweeping over the rest of Africa are combining to raise increasingly dangerous pressures, which for the moment are being forcibly repressed.

On an early summer day in December, white South Africans picnic and converse in a grove of large fir trees in a Cape Town suburb.

An Eden Claiming the Love of Its Divided Sons

South Africa is a harsh and spectacular country whose beauty inspires ardent devotion among its people. The terrain is varied and rugged, the climate temperate, the mineral resources seemingly unlimited. Although much of the political and social life of the country is characterized by discord, every faction feels equally wedded to this vast, impressive land. The interior is dominated by a great plateau, bordered to the east and south by a steep mountain range whose peaks slope abruptly down to the sea. Although farmers often suffer from a shortage of rain, nevertheless when there is a sudden downpour the earth springs into abundant life, sprouting a thousand varieties of flowers. Beneath the ground, gold, diamonds, uranium and coal wait to be added to the treasures already unearthed. The fertile acres of Natal and the open grasslands of the Transvaal cast a spell over all the citizens of South Africa—including the nonwhite majority whose lives have been so severely curtailed under the white man's rule.

RURAL LAND is the home of Africans who eke out a meager livelihood by farming and raising cattle

TRIBAL VILLAGE, where a girl covered with ritual powder *(left)* cooks as two young men battle with sticks, lies in the Transkei, the country's first African "homeland" to obtain limited self-government.

GRAZING LAND in the Transkei *(opposite)* rolls beyond a cluster of huts to the wooded hills. Because of overcrowding, limited fertility and overgrazing, most land in the tribal reserves is unproductive.

THATCHED HUTS surround turbaned Xhosa women in a kraal, or tribal village, in the Transkei. The Xhosa are a group of tribes who all speak the same language. Their homeland is in the Transkei, a territory about the size of Denmark in the eastern part of Cape Province. Native regions like the Transkei are an essential feature of the Government's plans for designating segregated areas as tribal homelands for the Africans. They comprise only about 13 per cent of the nation's area but officially are the permanent residences of nearly 70 per cent of the population.

NATURAL BEAUTY dwells in a stark landscape which offers scenes of imposing

grandeur and produces exotic vegetation

BRILLIANT BLOOM of a protea bush unfolds near the ocean in the southernmost part of the Cape of Good Hope. A larger species, the giant protea, is South Africa's national flower.

PLUNGING CASCADES of the Tugela River *(left)* roar below the amphitheater created by the Drakensberg range in Royal Natal National Park, a 20,000-acre flower and game sanctuary.

LUSH VINEYARDS in southwestern Cape Province, a region known for grapes and fine wines, are worked by two African laborers *(below)* under the supervision of a white foreman.

MODERN CITIES, crowded centers of commerce and industry, rise like mirages out of the land

STRIPED SPINNAKERS pull two sailboats along neck-and-neck in a race between rival yacht clubs in Durban. In the background are the chic hotels and shops of the city's Esplanade.

GOLD DUMPS outside Johannesburg *(right)*, the nation's largest city, provide a hilly playground for a group of boys. Nearly 80 years of mining has produced many such immense piles.

TALLEST BUILDING in South Africa, the Sanlam Insurance Building *(below, left)* rises above Cape Town in an area reclaimed from the sea. In the distance is famed Table Mountain.

BOER COMMEMORATION in Pretoria, the Day of the Covenant, brings forth Afrikaners in costume who pull an ox wagon. The festivities commemorate the Battle of Blood River on December 16, 1838, when the Boers dealt the Zulus a crushing blow.

2

Settling the Distant and Difficult Land

THE history of the settlement of South Africa begins with the arrival in Table Bay in April 1652 of three small vessels of the Dutch East India Company under the command of Jan van Riebeeck. The ships carried about 200 men in all, of whom some 80, along with a few women and children, would remain at Table Bay and form the nucleus of present-day Cape Town. They brought timber, tools, seeds for planting, guns and ammunition.

Their purpose, however, was not to found a colony but to establish a "refreshment station" which could provide meat and vegetables, water and repairs for vessels using the trade route round the southern point of Africa to the East Indies. This trade, which brought Europe its spices and silks—and huge profits to the traders—had been opened up by the Portuguese in the 15th Century; but with the decline of Portugal and Spain, it had been largely taken over by the Dutch.

Holland was now at the height of its greatness. Having thrown off the Spanish yoke in 1648 after 80 years of savage struggle, it had become one of the leading powers in Europe. Its trading fleet was the largest in the world, its mariners expert and adventurous. Its contacts with the East brought wealth and opened new windows onto unknown lands. Its universities and medical schools were renowned. It was dominant in the world of art and the intellect. But though the Eastern trade was rich, it was also dangerous—too dangerous for private venturers to carry the risk.

Before long, the small original trading companies had combined into the one great Dutch East India Company, with a charter from the Government. In the East, the Company's sway was absolute. It had its own army and navy, signed treaties and governed vast territories; it had its own judges who wielded powers of life and death. Details of the Company's operations were tightly guarded secrets. Its 17 directors were so closely interlocked with the rulers of the country that few questions about its activities were ever asked, or needed to be answered.

Van Riebeeck's orders were limiting and precise. There was no question of venturing far inland. He and his men were to build a fort, plant vegetable gardens for the benefit of scurvy-ridden crews, collect timber for ship repairs and barter for cattle with the inhabitants—with whom they were instructed to live at peace. These inhabitants they called the Hottentots. Dutch records describe them as crafty, thievish, idle and dirty. The Hottentots have left little record of their views about the Dutch, and drink and disease have today left very few Hottentots.

Certainly they resented being deprived of their grazing lands as the settlement expanded; they probably also resented being told how many of their cattle the newcomers required, and how much payment—usually in the form of copper—they would receive. In 1658 they resorted to war to defend their right of access to lands from which they were being steadily ousted, and their defeat, by the superior weapons and better organization of the Europeans, set the pattern for many such "wars" to come.

A YEAR before this first struggle with the African natives, in 1657, two events of great significance in the life of the settlement occurred. Nine employees of the Dutch East India Company took their discharges and settled down as "free burghers" on farmland allotted to them by the Company. These were the first true "Boers" in the history of South Africa. In the same year the first slaves were imported from Java and Madagascar.

Some historians believe that this last decision, to import slaves instead of seeking white laborers from Europe, was crucial for the future of the country—"perhaps the most fateful event in South African history." Had this not happened (so the argument runs), white laborers would inevitably have been brought in and South Africa would have been settled as were Canada, Australia and New Zealand. The sense of God-given superiority would not have developed in the whites—with its accompanying prejudices as to what is "white man's work" and what is "black man's work"—and the appalling problems of present-day South Africa might have been avoided, or at least reduced. "But having imported slaves," wrote Baron van Imhoff, Governor General of the Dutch Indies, who visited the Cape in 1743, "every common or ordinary European becomes a gentleman, and prefers to be served rather than to serve."

IT is easy, 300 years later, to see in the early settlement at the Cape seeds of all the problems that would later bedevil South Africa. The Dutch were representatives of a great monopoly, virtually answerable to no one for the way they carried out their orders. Their first contact in Africa was with the Hottentots, a poor and backward race, and when the Hottentots proved unreliable—and particularly after they had been decimated by smallpox in 1713—the settlers imported more slaves to do their donkey-work. In addition, the several months' voyage to Europe cut them off from new ideas in politics and religion, so that the settlers seem always to have been living in the mental climate of an earlier age.

All these circumstances have indeed influenced the course of South African history and the shape of the South African mind. But to suppose that the coming clash of races could have been avoided by the importation of more whites in the early days, or by a refusal to import slaves, is to overlook the existence—behind and beyond the territories ranged over by the diminished Hottentot bands—of the great tribes of Bantu peoples, whose descendants constitute today nearly 13 million of the 19 million human beings living in South Africa. The most powerful actor in South Africa's drama could not permanently have remained off stage.

In the last quarter of the 17th Century, the Dutch East India Company changed its policy. Instead of regarding the Cape merely as a "refreshment station" manned by Company employees, it wished to make it more of a colony and thus more capable of self-defense. Its strategic position on the route to the East was giving Cape Town, in an age of almost continuous European warfare, much greater importance than had been foreseen. Free passage was offered to new settlers from Holland, and Company employees who had served their time were encouraged by a grant of land to stay on as burghers.

Under an energetic commander, Simon van der Stel, sent out in 1679, the settlement began to grow. There were nine free burghers in 1657, 64 in 1672 and 573 in 1687, and in 1688 came 200 French Huguenots who brought a useful knowledge of wine cultivation. Though the use of French was discouraged by the Dutch and the language died out, their names—Du Toit, Du Plessis, Theron and others—are among the commonest in South Africa today. By 1708, a little over half a century after the "refreshment station" was founded, there were 1,700 free burghers and 1,250 slaves living in the Cape, together with some hundreds of Company officials and a medley of Hottentots and people of mixed race.

AS their numbers grew, trade with the occasional visiting vessel became ever less profitable. The East India Company's price-fixing and other restrictions on this trade denied the farmers a fair return for their produce. Nor was there any more room in the sheltered valleys near Cape Town. Farmers and farmers' sons began to push out north into the interior and eastward along the coast. Here the farmers turned naturally to cattle ranching, which promised them economic independence. At first the land was free; after 1714, a small yearly payment would lease a farm of 6,000 acres. Many farmers occupied several, "selling" their old ones when the pasture began to be exhausted and moving farther on over the mountains or along the coast.

This migration brought these "trekboers"—or farmers-on-the-move—into conflict with the Bushmen. The Bushmen were a small and primitive people, living a nomadic Stone Age life, hunting for game with poisoned arrows and living in flimsy huts or caves. They were also resolute warriors in defense of their hunting grounds and water holes.

To the trekboers, these Bushmen were dangerous pests, and they exterminated them in organized shooting parties. Jacob Abraham de Mist, who was sent out to the Cape as Commissioner General about 1803, spoke of these hunts regretfully as "teaching our people to shoot down a fellow-being with as little compunction as they would a hare or wolf." Not unnaturally, the life of the trekboers developed in them the attitude that a man has the natural right to as much land as he wants, with a constant supply of labor on his own terms, and that the duty of a government is either to clear any occupying peoples out of his path or leave him free to do so in his own way.

WHILE the trekboers were moving farther and farther into the interior, events were taking shape in Europe which would vitally affect the whole pattern of life and government in South Africa. In 1794 a French Revolutionary Army marched into the Low Countries, and the Dutch Prince, William of Orange, fled to England to form a Government-in-Exile. The British were members of the alliance fighting France, and the British Admiralty saw the necessity of keeping the strategic harbor of Table Bay out of the hands of the French Navy. Supported and given legal sanction by William of Orange, the British occupied Cape Town in September 1795.

This first British occupation, which lasted seven and a half years, introduced few changes and was not unpopular. In 1803 the British withdrew, but in 1806 they were back, war with France having broken out again. In 1814 their stay was ratified by treaty. And so, some 150 years after van Riebeeck's landing, control of the Cape passed out of Dutch hands and into British, where it was to remain for the next 150, before being taken over by a new breed of men descended from the Dutch—the Afrikaners.

What the British took over at the start of the 19th Century was a loosely organized, ill-defined settlement of 25,000 Europeans, 30,000 slaves, and perhaps another 20,000 Hottentots, Malays, Coloreds of mixed blood, and freed and escaped slaves. In the whole area, only three administrative centers outside Cape Town had been set up. Trade was small and the currency in complete confusion, every kind of money being in circulation at values that continually varied. Justice, in the sense of access to law, was virtually for whites alone. Title to land in many parts of the country was insecure, farms having simply been occupied, then sold and sold again without any legal formalities. The trekboers were in constant dispute with the Cape authorities. Legally, economically and from the point of view of an effective administration, the colony was not far from chaos. Moreover, on the undefined frontiers, there was the prospect of far graver troubles.

WHILE the Government of the Cape was changing hands, the trekboers in the interior had been increasingly coming in contact with another new people. Far more advanced, far better organized, far stronger in physique than either the Hottentots or the Bushmen, the Bantu had been moving southward from lands near the heart of Africa for hundreds of years, driven down by the search for new pastures and by the ceaseless slave-raiding of the Arabs from the north.

Like the trekboers, the Bantu (a name given to the Negroes inhabiting most of Africa south of the equator who speak about 200 related languages and dialects) were cattle farmers. Like the trekboers, they were driven onward under pressure of the need for new grazing land. These two pressures would leave the two races, after a dozen border wars and endless minor skirmishes, deeply interlocked in what is today the Republic of South Africa.

The Bantu people with whom the trekboers principally came into contact were the Xhosa. Like the Boers, they were agricultural and pastoral. For reasons deeply rooted in their social customs, their culture and their religion, they set an exceedingly high value on cattle. Moreover, they were a politically developed people, capable of prolonged resistance even in the face of the superior weapons and greater resources of the whites. For a century, from about 1780 to 1880, there was almost constant border warfare. The British Government in the Cape, like the governors of the East India Company before them, continually sought to fix boundaries beyond which neither trekboer nor Xhosa cattlemen would venture. But neither Government had the resources in men or money to establish a guarded frontier and enforce the respect of both parties for it.

The trekboers accused the Xhosa of murderous and barbaric raids, of slaughtering women and children and of cattle rustling. The Xhosa accused the trekboers of endless aggression and disregard of the agreements made for them by their governments in Cape Town. Moreover, all boundary settlements were constantly being nullified by the different meanings attached to them by the two parties. The whites understood such agreements as entitling them to the *possession* of land, in perpetuity, to do with as they pleased. The tribesmen thought they were parting with the *use* of the land, and that such parting could be revocable. Both sides also resorted to trickery, and felt free to do so because of what they considered the trickery of their opponents.

These "Kaffir Wars," as they were called, continued right up to 1877, and on whatever pretext they were started, their effect was the extension of the territories occupied by the whites at the expense of those occupied by the blacks. This steady, and bloody, white encroachment is pictured rather differently by the history textbooks used in South Africa's Government-supervised schools. These textbooks show the Boer farmer as longing only for a peaceful life while he is constantly attacked by hordes of murderous savages.

WHOEVER was at fault in these wars, and whoever benefited, the fighting went on and the borders were in a constant state of flux. In such a situation, the British, with their passion for organization, their insistence on orderly rule as the basis of prosperity through trade, and their conviction that the sooner everyone else made use of the English language the better for all concerned, were soon at loggerheads with the Dutch colonists. The Dutch could tolerate, and even welcome, the stabilization of the currency. Economic measures which brought about a sixfold increase in imports and exports in 14 years had at least an agreeable side. Good roads and bridges, a lighthouse, a public library and pipe-borne water in Cape Town—even an influx of Scottish schoolmasters who first established schools and finally a college—might be accepted. But there were other changes much less tolerable to the Dutch.

The British established circuit courts, at which not only could one farmer bring a law case against another, but a Hottentot servant could complain of ill-treatment by his master. One such complaint, in 1815, has become famous. A Hottentot servant brought a charge of cruelty against a farmer named Bezuidenhout. When Bezuidenhout treated with contempt a summons to answer these charges, a white officer came to arrest him, accompanied by 12 Hottentot soldiers. Such a thing had never been known, and Bezuidenhout fired on the party and was killed in the subsequent skirmish. His brother and some friends swore vengeance and sought the help of a Xhosa chief to set up their own republic. Their revolt soon failed and five of the rebels were hanged, after trial by a British court, at a place known as Slagter's Nek, a name still charged with deep emotion for many South Africans.

The new legal system, and the arrival of a number of missionaries who were sponsored by the London Missionary Society, changed the whole basis of life at the Cape. The missionaries regarded the Hottentots and slaves not primarily as labor but as souls for salvation. They were imbued with the new ideas of equality which were spreading throughout Europe, and being men of vigor and determination, they were also in many cases tactless and unappreciative of local difficulties.

In the early years of British occupation, legislation was still enforced which made it difficult for a Hottentot to leave his district, and bound his children as "apprentices" to his employer. The Reverend Dr. John Philip, who came out in 1819, was determined to relieve the Hottentots of all such disabilities and by 1828 had secured the passing of the "Hottentot Charter," placing them on an all but equal footing with whites. In 1834 came the liberation of all slaves—a noble measure, but one that embittered the slaveowners, who received far less compensation than they expected. The agitation leading to these measures made missionaries such as Dr. Philip detested in their lifetimes and the objects of bitter criticism to the present day.

Nor was this all. In 1820, with the assistance of the Government in London, some 5,000 British immigrants came out and were settled in the Zuurveld, close to the Fish River. They were glad to get away from the misery and unemployment at home which followed the Napoleonic wars, and the Cape Government was glad to settle them on the colony's boundary as an economical measure of defense. The scheme was ill-planned, and many of the settlers soon drifted away to the towns, where, however, their industrial skills and commercial experience enabled most of them to make a living.

Five thousand settlers, of course, made a considerable difference in the make-up of a white population which numbered before their arrival only about 40,000. They were English-speaking and were imbued with the habits and ideas of their homeland. Their coming rendered easier the introduction in 1828 of a measure, unwise as well as unpopular, which made English the only official language. A complete and necessary revision of the whole judicial system took place at the same time. In 1828 also—after a long struggle led by Thomas Pringle and John Fairbairn—freedom of the press was established. Meanwhile, the slow process leading to representative government had been begun. In 1825 a Council of Advice was instituted, replaced in 1834 by a Legislative Council. A system of local government was initiated and the method of land holding regularized. Crown lands in the future were to be sold at auction instead of simply being occupied by the trekboers for rents which were always trivial and frequently unpaid.

All these legal and administrative changes might well have been enough to cause disaffection among the Dutch colonists, but the liberation of the slaves and legal rights for nonwhites were for many of them

SOME SOUTH AFRICAN TERMS

The first South African colonists called themselves *burghers*, the old Dutch word for citizens. *Boer*, a term for the Dutch-descended South Africans which was used increasingly in the 19th Century, means simply "farmer." It is sometimes still used today, but has been largely replaced by *Afrikaner* (pronounced Afri-KAHN-er), which means "African." As a result, the Dutch-descended Afrikaners object when other people use "African" to mean black men—as do the black Africans themselves. The Afrikaners use the words *Bantu* or *Kaffir* for the blacks. *Bantu*, which literally means "people," is today the South African Government's official term for all black Africans in the country. *Kaffir* carries a distinctly derogatory overtone for Africans; it originally derives from an Arab word meaning "infidel."

the last straw. In the middle 1830s, thousands of Dutch farmers, mainly from among the trekboers, made up their minds to get away from the hated British rule. They loaded all they could carry onto their ox wagons and trekked north into the interior, where they could occupy as much land as they pleased and live in accordance with nobody's beliefs, opinions or regulations but their own.

Before setting out, one of the leaders of the Great Trek, Piet Retief, drew up a manifesto giving the reasons for their action. "We quit this colony under the full assurance that the English government has nothing more to require of us, and will allow us to govern ourselves without its interference in future." He went on to complain of the laws giving rights to Hottentots and Coloreds, the heavy losses imposed by the liberation of slaves, the dangers to which farmers and their families were exposed in the frontier districts, and the activities of the missionaries, whom he characterized as "interested and dishonest persons, whose testimony, under the cloak of religion, is believed in England to the exclusion of all evidence in our favor."

The reasons given by a woman trekker, Anna Steenkamp—in the depth of racial feeling they reveal, and the passionate conviction that such feeling is not only right but divinely inspired and ordained—could be paralleled many times over in the writings and utterances of the Afrikaners of today. She blames ". . . the shameful and unjust proceedings with reference to the freeing of our slaves; and yet it is not so much their freeing which drove us to such lengths, as their being placed on an equal footing with Christians, contrary to the laws of God, and the natural distinction of race and color, so that it was intolerable for any decent Christian to bow beneath such a yoke; wherefore we rather withdrew in order thus to preserve our doctrines in purity."

THE years usually given for the Great Trek are 1836 to 1838, but parties were setting out as early as 1835, and for a year or two beforehand, scouts had been spying out the land to the north and northeast. The scouts brought back glowing accounts of the lush grass and the vast open spaces, almost empty of "Kaffirs," which would be theirs for the taking. Louis Trigardt and Janse van Rensburg were the first leaders to set out, each with a small group of half a dozen families with their horses, cattle, sheep and goats. Each family had one or two wagons drawn by 12 or 16 oxen, and they moved slowly northward over what is now the Orange Free State and the Transvaal, far up into the Zoutpansberg not far from the Limpopo River.

BUT the same spirit of independence and rejection of compromise which had led the trekkers to set out led them also to disagree. Trigardt and van Rensburg quarreled, as other trek leaders would continually do later. Van Rensburg went east, making for Delagoa Bay in Portuguese territory—and disappeared with all his company on the way. Trigardt, after spending some time in the Zoutpansberg, also started over the Drakensberg range toward the east coast. There were, of course, no roads. Finding a route through the mountains involved terrible struggle and hardship. Wagons had to be taken to pieces and reassembled again and again. When they finally reached the lowlands, Trigardt's party suffered from malaria and their cattle were attacked by the tsetse fly. Only a small remnant finally reached Natal three years after they had set out from the Cape.

Two other leaders, Hendrik Potgieter and Sarel Cilliers, set off in 1836 with larger parties. Having crossed the present Orange Free State, Potgieter succeeded in obtaining the land between the Vet and Vaal Rivers from a chief of the Bataung tribe in return for protection against the warlike Matabele people.

Potgieter soon had occasion to live up to his part of the bargain, for the Matabele attacked his wagon train at a hill still known as the Vegkop, or Battle Hill. There he prepared to meet the enemy by arranging what was to become the Boers' standard method of defense against the spear-throwing Bantu—a method which is still of great symbolic potency for the Afrikaner. He formed a "laager," or circle of wagons, the gaps between them stuffed with thorn bushes, and an inner laager of four wagons for the women and children. From this protection he and about 40 men and boys were able to beat off all the enemy's attacks. Potgieter lost indeed all his sheep and cattle, and the loss of the oxen

AN EPIC MIGRATION known as the Great Trek (1836-1838) led to the settlement of South Africa's interior by the Boers. These Dutch-descended farmers had previously spread eastward from Cape Town along the south coastal plain, but hostile African tribes (Xhosa, Tembu, etc.) interfered with further expansion. In the 1830s, increasingly impatient with British rule from Cape Town, the Boers decided to go north in search of new land. Following the routes shown, they crossed the Orange River and established temporary headquarters at Thaba Nchu before attempting to cross the Drakensberg range to the fertile region around Port Natal. The only African tribes to give them trouble were the Matabele and the Zulu (shaded areas). Two battles—Vegkop and Mosega—were fought with the Matabele; then in 1838, Piet Retief and some of his men were massacred by the Zulu leader, Dingaan. Later, the Boers avenged themselves by savagely defeating the Zulus at Blood River. Although by 1839 all the original leaders except Potgieter were dead, the trek itself continued on a lesser scale until the 1850s, by which time several Boer republics were established in the areas that had been traversed by the trekkers.

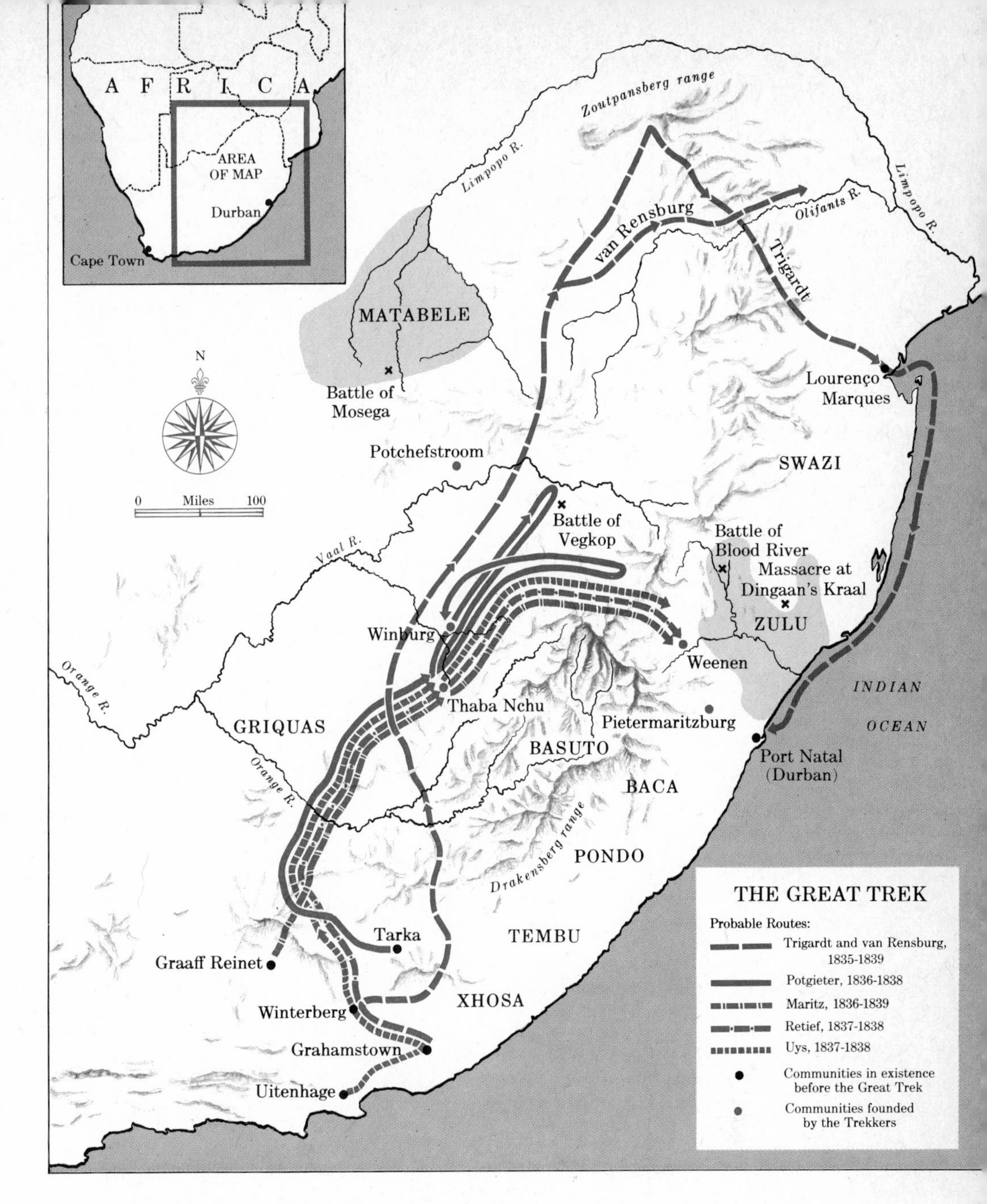

rendered him immobile, but the horses were inside and he was able to summon help from a place called Thaba Nchu to the south, where other parties of trekkers were assembling.

By July 1837, more than 2,000 trekkers had collected at Thaba Nchu and a simple form of government had been organized. Piet Retief was to be Governor, with Gerrit Maritz as Chairman of the Volksraad, or Council. There were endless quarrels, however, as to the direction they should take, and when in August, Retief, Maritz and their followers set off for Natal, Potgieter and another leader, Piet Uys, refused to follow.

Natal appeared to Retief's followers to be indeed the promised land they were seeking. Leaving his main body of followers in the Drakensberg passes with orders to await his return, Retief approached the Zulu ruler, Dingaan, for permission to settle on some of his land.

Dingaan received Retief with an appearance of courtesy, merely asking him to recover some stolen cattle, but in fact he was highly suspicious. He had heard of the defeat of the Matabele and of the power of the Boers' muzzle-loading flintlocks. Moreover, contrary to Retief's instructions, the main body of trekkers with 1,000 wagons was already across the mountains and streaming down the valleys into Dingaan's territory. Despite warnings of danger, Retief, with 70 Boer followers and 30 Hottentots, accepted Dingaan's invitation to attend a goodwill banquet in the royal kraal. At a cry from Dingaan of "Kill the wizards!" Retief and his followers were seized by Zulu warriors, dragged to a nearby hill and clubbed to death. Dingaan then sent his men to attack the straggling and unprepared trekkers who had come down the face of the Drakensberg, killing 500 of them and carrying off their cattle.

DESPITE these reverses, the remaining Boers did not withdraw. They reorganized their forces and established a small state around a newly founded township which they later named Pietermaritzburg, after their leaders Piet Retief and Gerrit Maritz. There they were joined by another famous trek leader, Andries Pretorius, from whom Pretoria would later take its name. This combined force of Boers made preparations to revenge themselves on Dingaan. After advancing into Zululand for several days, they formed a laager in a strong position on the banks of the Blood River. There, on December 16, 1838, the Zulus attacked. It was a one-sided battle. Wave after wave of the Zulus was shot down. In all, 3,000 of Dingaan's warriors were killed at the cost of three Boers slightly wounded. Further expeditions against Dingaan, in which the Boers had the support of Dingaan's half brother Panda and a large force of Zulus, finally shattered his power.

And so, three years after the first parties had set out, the trekkers had reached their goal and established a republic known as Natalia on the fertile slopes leading down to the coast of the Indian Ocean.

The story of the Great Trek is told here in some detail because of its deep and continuing importance to the Afrikaner people and the profound effect it has had on their character. To the Afrikaner, the Great Trek is the heroic epic of his people, in which a nation was formed and found itself in the face of danger. It is more meaningful to him than the conquest of the West is to a citizen of the United States, or the defeat of the Spanish Armada is to a Briton. In the words of a leading Afrikaner teacher: "The Great Trek is regarded by the Afrikaner as the point on which the whole history of South Africa pivots." Much of the Afrikaner's thinking is still colored by its events, impressed on him over and over again throughout his school days and re-enacted for him in pageants and folklore.

Partly because of Dingaan's treachery, black people in mass tend to be looked upon as untrustworthy and savage, constituting a *swart gevaar,* or black menace, against which the leader and his people protect themselves by going into laager and presenting an unbroken front. Not to join the laager, not to take one's place among the *volk* in thinking and acting just as they do, is not merely to disagree —it is to leave one's post unguarded and to be responsible for the enemy gaining access to the fortress. Equally, to propose any form of compromise is to invite trickery and destruction from a cunning and ruthless foe.

A week before the battle of Blood River, one of the trek leaders vowed that if God would grant victory, a church would be built and the day of the victory held sacred. Now, on each December 16, the anniversary of the battle of Blood River (officially known as The Day of the Covenant), political and religious leaders remind the *volk* of their covenant with God, of the menaces they still have to face, and of the need for absolute unity and cohesion. More than 100 years after the battle, on December 16, 1949, the Afrikaner people dedicated a colossal monument to the trekkers on a hill above Pretoria; the laager of ox wagons carved in relief around its base forms one of the most revealing symbols of the spirit of Afrikanerdom.

ON this subject of the Great Trek, as on the whole history of South Africa, the opinion of the African himself is seldom heard; he has written few historical accounts, and there survives almost no contemporary record of what his people thought and felt. But at a meeting of the African National Congress in 1949, a speaker referred to the Great Trek as "a gigantic plunder expedition, besmirched with the blood of innocent natives." This may indeed be overstated. But many an African must have had the experience recorded by a chief in the Transvaal: "My grandfather woke one morning at his own kraal and found a white man who said, 'You are living on my farm and you must work for me.' "

Members of Cape Town's Colored population, who are of mixed African, Asian and European stock, march in the Coon Carnival.

Layers of Peoples in a Rigidly Segregated Society

The population of South Africa is stratified in layers formed by distinct ethnic groups, and the Government with its segregation policies strives to keep each group intact. The largest group is made up of the Africans, who had begun migrating into the region by 1500. In the 17th Century, Dutch colonists settled on the Cape of Good Hope; they formed the nucleus of today's Afrikaners (South Africans of Dutch descent). Miscegenation over the centuries between the Europeans, imported Southeast Asian slaves and indigenous tribes produced the Coloreds *(above)*. The Cape Colony became a British possession in 1814 and began to attract British settlers. Finally, in the 1860s white planters in Natal brought indentured servants from India, the ancestors of South Africa's present Asian population.

THE WHITES enjoy a high standard of living and numerous special privileges

EUROPEAN PRESERVE, Sea Point, a wealthy suburb of Cape Town, stretches along the Atlantic seashore, where children play in the sun. The home of rich white immigrants from all over Europe and Africa, Sea Point has modern hotels and apartment houses as well as landscaped parks and gardens. Under the Group Areas Act, nonwhites are forbidden to live in Sea Point.

ENGLISH SCHOOL, the Durban Girls' College, a primary and secondary institution, releases a stream of girls. All white students in South Africa must learn both English and Afrikaans.

AFRIKANER CEREMONY in Cape Town reaches a solemn moment *(below)* as an Afrikaner official lays a wreath below a statue of Jan van Riebeeck, the Dutch founder of Cape Town.

BALANCING FIREWOOD, women of the Nyanda tribe sing as they walk along a Transkei road. Most Transkei residents are women, children and old people, since the young men leave to work in the mines and factories.

PERFORMING A DANCE, an African mineworker *(below)* takes part in a contest at Crown Mines, Limited. Mine owners hold the competitions to entertain the African miners and to help preserve tribal individuality.

THE AFRICANS observe their folk customs despite the decline of tribal life

SHOPPING FOR GOODS, two Baca women in tribal dress come to the Saturday market in Richmond, a town in southern Natal. Since the woman at right is a recent bride and has just had her first child, the beaded knob over her forehead is small. As she grows older and gives birth to more children, she will make the headdress larger to indicate her increasing status.

THE INDIANS preserve their cultural identity while seeking security and equality in their adopted country

HINDU CEREMONY in a middle-class Indian home in a Durban suburb *(left)* seals the engagement of a young couple. The two fathers, to the left of the couple, also take part. On the floor are symbolic flowers and powders surrounding an oil lamp which stands for the life-giving sun.

INFORMAL MOMENT brings together the newly engaged couple *(below)* with their families after the ceremony. More than 236,000 Indians live in Durban. Many are poor, but some are prosperous merchants or professional people despite Government limitations on their activities.

FASHION SHOW during an Indian sports day outside Durban features Indian girls modeling saris. Detested by many Africans as exploiters, the Indians have retreated into exclusiveness. A clash between Africans and Asians shook Durban in 1949.

LAUGHING WOMEN race on the annual sports day. Though relatively well off, Indians often support African demands for rights. Indian protest was first voiced by Gandhi, who led "passive resistance" in South Africa before his drive in India.

REFINED GOLD BARS, valued at $14,000 each, blaze in the sun as they are transported within the grounds of the Rand Refinery in Johannesburg. South Africa produces more than half the world's gold, and refined 30.9 million ounces in 1966.

3

Change Wrought by Gold and Diamonds

THE history of the Great Trek (see Chapter 2) does not end with the defeat of Dingaan and the trekkers' descent, with their battered wagons and decimated flocks, into the fertile "promised land" of Natal. After heavy loss of life and fearful hardships the trekkers had finally reached their goal—only to find that their old enemies, the British, from whom they had been trying so desperately to escape, had arrived there first. British traders and a garrison of British troops were already established in Port Natal (later to become Durban), the one magnificent natural harbor in 800 miles of coastline. Within four years of its establishment, the trekker republic of Natalia, in 1843, was formally made a British colony by the Government in London.

It is not surprising that the Afrikaner attitude towards the British should have contained—and contains to the present day—a strong admixture of exasperation. The people of Dutch descent had spent a century and a half establishing themselves in the Cape. Progress had not been fast, but it had been at the rate they liked and in the direction they preferred. Then the British arrived and took over. In less than 30 years—with their interfering missionaries and their insistence on what they called justice—they had so upset the established order that thousands of Boer farmers were prepared to sell their properties and most of their belongings, as we have seen, and trek off with whatever they could carry into the unknown. After having finally reached their goal and turned defeat into victory, they suddenly found themselves once more thwarted by the British.

Rather than accept the rule of the hated British in Natal, many of the outraged veterans of the Trek once more hitched up their ox wagons and started back over the Drakensberg range, settling precariously between the Orange River and the Vaal and then moving north to new lands beyond the Vaal. There, at last, the aims of the trekkers seemed to lie within their grasp. By the Sand River Convention of 1852, the independence of the Boers north of the Vaal was recognized and a republic established. (Officially called the South African Republic, it continued to be known by its geographical name, the Transvaal.) Two years later, in 1854, the Boers living between the Vaal and the Orange became independent and organized another Boer republic, the Orange Free State.

THROUGHOUT this period two tendencies were at work shaping the country's future. First, there was a tendency on the part of the passionately independent Boers to split up into ever smaller groups. At one time, in the year 1857, there were actually no fewer than eight separate governments in South Africa—five Boer republics and three British colonies. But there was an opposite tendency to federate and unify, sparked mainly by the British desire for prosperity and orderliness. This latter tendency received a tremendous impetus in the third quarter of the century from two great mineral discoveries—of gold and diamonds. The profound changes wrought by these discoveries not only intensified the antagonism between Boer and Briton, giving rise eventually to the armed strife known as the Boer War (see Chapter 4), but also established the basis for both political unification and for the economic pattern still in existence today.

Diamonds were discovered first. Originally they were found in quantity along the banks of the Vaal River, where even today a hundred or so prospectors still make an arduous living, washing and sieving the red soil. Word of the discovery traveled fast, and during 1868 and 1869 prospectors and fortune hunters began to pour into the area not only from all over South Africa but also from Britain, Australia, America and Europe. In 1870 and 1871, the flow became a flood when it was learned that there were many more diamonds in the "dry diggings" in and around what would soon be called Kimberley than there were on the riverbanks. By the end of the year 1871, Kimberley—previously a barren slope—had become the second largest town in South Africa. Output grew rapidly, and within 10 years, $100 million worth of diamonds had been mined.

IT soon became clear that the diamond finds were not merely a matter of lucky prospectors picking up prizes, but that a new and lasting source of wealth had been uncovered. Before long two problems loomed. The first, an immediate one, was the question of who had control over the land, the Boers or the British? The second, which followed a few years later, was the problem of how mining was to be organized so that a confusion of conflicting claims, fluctuating prices and inefficient digging might be avoided and diamond mining develop into a large-scale industry.

Kimberley and the surrounding area lay on the ill-defined border between the Orange Free State and a territory known as Griqualand West, which was occupied by a chief named Waterboer and his people, who were of mixed white and Hottentot origin. In 1870 Waterboer applied for British protection, which was granted. The British claim to the Kimberley district rested largely on this request that they come in and administer Griqualand West. But the Orange Free State had a claim as well, based on its having succeeded to the territories of the Orange River Sovereignty, a former British administrative unit which had included the disputed lands. A third claim was put in by the Transvaal, but this had little serious foundation.

After much argument and unrest, Sir Henry Barkly, the Governor of the Cape, decided that the dispute had to be settled by arbitration, and he chose Robert William Keate, the British Lieutenant Governor of Natal, as arbitrator. Today it is generally accepted that the Orange Free State's claim was the strongest and most firmly based. However, Keate gave his decision in favor of Waterboer—and thus of Britain. The area was annexed to the Cape Colony, and $450,000 was later paid to the Free State by Britain as compensation.

The second problem—the consolidation of the individual claims into a single great mining corporation—would bring to the fore some of the most striking figures in South African history.

Cecil John Rhodes was born in England in 1853, the son of a Hertfordshire parson. He had come out to South Africa in 1870 at the age of 17 because he was threatened with tuberculosis. At 18 he went to work in the diamond fields. Here the dry air suited him. The ill-health by which he was harassed all his life was overcome for the time. His digging prospered, and he was soon so successful that he was able to send himself to Oxford, where, after eight years of commuting between Britain and South Africa, he finally took his degree.

Numbers of books have been written about Cecil Rhodes, and many more no doubt will yet be written. He was a puzzle to the men of his own day, and he remains, if anything, more of a puzzle after the biographies have been read. In two respects particularly Rhodes is an enigma. He appears to have had much less than the normal human need for emotional and physical relationships, yet he possessed the power of attracting strong affection and devotion from those around him. Though he was awkward, nervously restless, far from good-looking and often blunt to the point of rudeness, and though he had little regard for anyone else's views or feelings—his conversations being mainly monologues—he could, when he exerted himself, charm convinced opponents and hardened men of the world into letting him have his way, often against their interests as well as inclinations.

IN the single-minded pursuit of his dream—an African continent ruled by Britain—he was unscrupulous to the point of trickery. In one way or another he deceived almost everyone who trusted him, from the shareholders in his companies to Jan Hendrik Hofmeyr and the Afrikaners of the Cape, who believed he was working with them for a unified, self-governing South Africa. And yet, today he is almost universally described and remembered as a great man, who did more than any other to bring the dark continent of Africa into the modern world.

In minor ways also his character is full of contradictions. He pursued money with remorseless concentration. "Money is power," he often said, and he made himself a millionaire before he was 30 and Prime Minister of the Cape at 37. He declared that "every man has his price," frequently invited an opponent to name his and paid it on the spot. But his own tastes were the simplest and his manner of dressing was casual to the point of being disreputable. Even his enemies admitted that he did not value money for its own sake but for what he believed that in his hands it could achieve.

CLOSELY associated with Rhodes was a man whom no one could accuse of greatness or nobility, yet who was in many ways more likable and human. Barney Barnato was the son of a shopkeeper in London's slum area called Whitechapel. At 14 he had made his living selling old clothes from a handbarrow in Petticoat Lane. Before he came to South Africa in the diamond rush he had been juggler, acrobat and clown. Wandering around the Kimberley diggings with a broken-down pony and cart, he soon got to know all he needed to know about diamonds and about the value of other men's claims.

Having accumulated a small capital of $15,000, Barnato began to buy land. Diamonds in the early days had been found in what was called "yellow ground"—yellowish clay near the surface of ancient "volcanic pipes" (outlets within volcanoes through which the molten rock escapes). The yellow clay only went down a short way, and by 1876 it was becoming worked out. Diggers were reaching the "blue ground" which lay below, then packing up and clearing off.

Barney Barnato believed, as did a few geologists also, that the blue ground was where diamonds in quantity would be found. Blue ground was indeed simply yellow ground which had not made contact with the atmosphere, and Barnato's hunch proved right. Four years later he was making nearly $10,000 a week and using the money to invest in still more claims. However, working the blue ground meant going down hundreds of feet into separate claims that were sometimes only a few yards across, and conditions rapidly became chaotic. Shaft walls collapsed. Roadways fell into the workings. Accidents

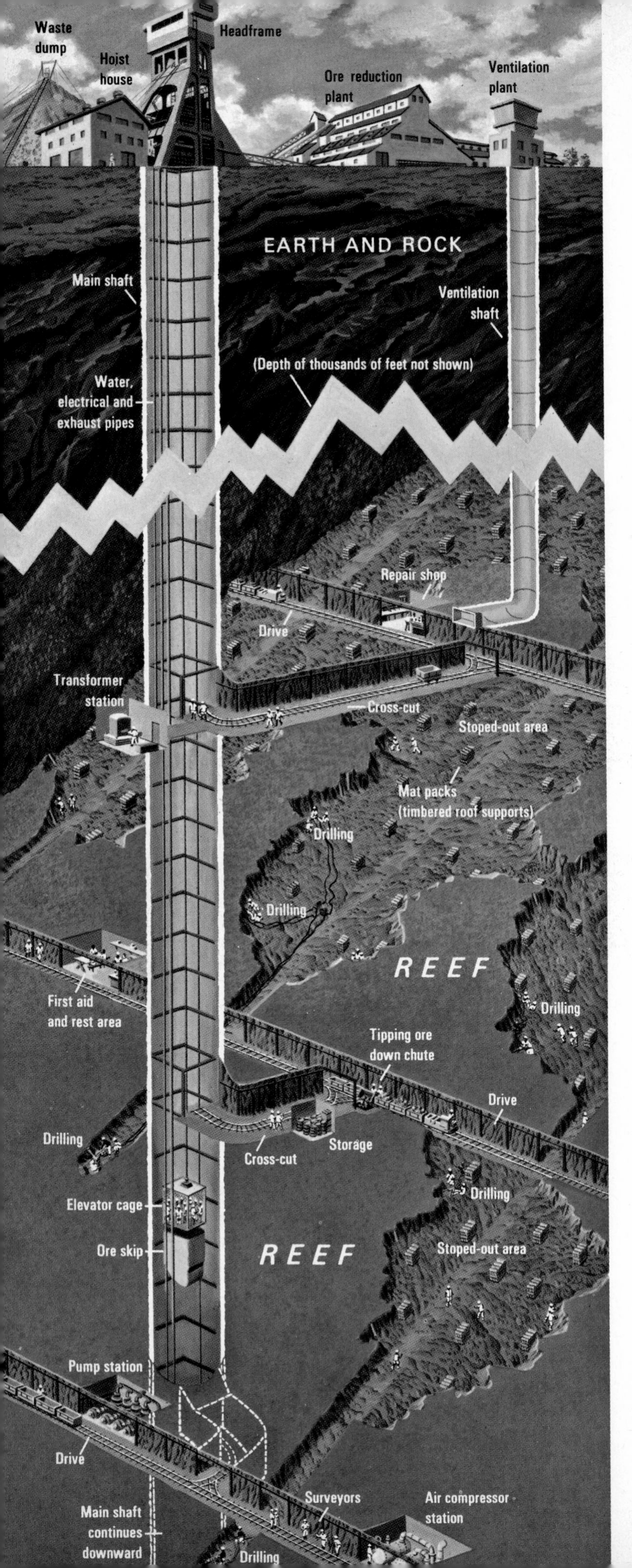

happened almost daily, and there were endless quarrels over rights. Meantime, through ill-organized marketing, the price of diamonds fell.

Both Barnato and Rhodes, who had become fierce competitors in the diamond industry, soon seized on the same idea—amalgamation, consolidation and finally monopoly. Barnato was the stronger financially, but Rhodes the more persistent. After a financial battle of the giants—and a final 18 hours of nonstop bargaining—De Beers Consolidated Mines was formed with Rhodes as chairman. One of the checks which changed hands in the transaction was for £5,338,650 (about $26 million). It is still preserved in the head offices of De Beers in Kimberley.

But the soil of South Africa had only yielded up the smaller part of its riches. In 1884, four years before Rhodes bought out Barnato, gold was discovered in the Transvaal on the Witwatersrand (Ridge of White Waters). Prospectors had known for some time that gold was present in the area, but now it had definitely been located, and in large quantities. A gold rush soon began beside which the earlier diamond rush was a mere scramble. All over the world men abandoned their jobs, said goodbye to their families and set off for the bare uplands south of Pretoria. Where there had been nothing but an empty hillside there was soon a vast, sprawling mining camp; in 10 years the mining camp had become a city of 100,000 people, which, in turn, was the center of a complex of smaller towns stretching for miles along the Reef. (Reef, which is the geologist's term for a gold-bearing stratum of rock, soon came to serve as the name of the whole gold-mining area.) Today the mining camp is Johannesburg, a city of more than a million inhabitants, black and white, and the biggest metropolis in Africa except for Cairo.

A TYPICAL GOLD MINE, shown in the cutaway drawing at left, is virtually an underground city in which thousands of men labor far beneath the earth's surface—sometimes more than two miles down. All mines have a main shaft (for personnel and supplies) and a ventilation shaft. From the main shaft, tunnels called "cross-cuts" lead to the reef—the thin, slanting layer of gold-bearing ore. Lateral tunnels, or "drives," lead to passageways that slant up or down along the face of the reef. Drilling and blasting operations gradually enlarge these passageways to form huge underground rooms called "stoped-out areas." New ore is taken in diesel trains to chutes leading to the ore skip, a large elevator-mounted bucket which brings it to the surface.

Gold mining on the Reef was very different from seeking diamonds at Kimberley. The gold lay at a great depth. Very deep shafts had to be driven—in recent years some have gone two miles down—and from the outset costly machinery was needed to extract the ore. There was no room for the individual prospector; no room soon for the small company, of which at one time there were more than 450. Amalgamations rapidly thinned these out into a small number of powerful groups. No individual digger could pick up fortunes on the Reef, but there was work for any man with strength or skill, and most of those who had arrived stayed on.

Rhodes refused at first to be interested in the gold fields. He had just begun his battle for amalgamation of the diamond industry and was reluctant to embark on a fresh undertaking. The most he would do was to let an acquaintance with a mere $1,000 in expense money buy options on farms below which gold might be found. Before long his friends persuaded him to become more seriously involved, but Rhodes never dominated the gold industry as he did that of diamonds. His interest in the area was to be mainly political, and his ambition to force the Transvaal under the British flag made inevitable his clash with Paul Kruger, the shrewd and able President of the Transvaal, a patriarchal figure who epitomizes for every Afrikaner the patience, courage and stubbornness of their people (see Chapter 4).

THE discoveries of gold and diamonds completely transformed the country and its future. South Africa had been until then a pastoral and poverty-stricken land whose dominating figure was the farmer, white or black. Its main products were wool, wine, meat and, to a lesser extent, wheat. The overwhelming majority of its people—including many whites—scarcely made use of money. They grew what they needed and made their own clothes. Life was bounded by their farms or kraals, and their infrequent journeys were by ox wagon, on horseback or on foot. A trip every three months to a small town for *nagmaal*—Holy Communion—was the big event in the life of most Boer families.

The finding of mineral wealth, with the new prosperity which quickly followed, vibrated over the whole country, shaking the old pastoral life to pieces. Hundreds of thousands of immigrants were attracted, many of a type different from, and highly unwelcome to, the existing communities. Following these newcomers came railroads. The 70 miles of local rail lines—all that existed in the whole of South Africa in 1871—were soon extended to form, within 20 years, a network covering the entire land. Roads were driven across mountains, bridges were built and telegraph lines were strung, linking town with town. The most stagnant of colonial regions suddenly exploded into activity, and the foundations were laid for an industrial economy comparable to those of Europe and America.

The pay envelopes for an ever-increasing number of workers and mine officials created a new demand for produce and goods of all kinds. Agricultural prices soared—eggs reached a peak of five dollars a dozen at Kimberley—and farmers consequently benefited. Imports and exports rose sharply in the Cape, Natal, the Transvaal and the Orange Free State. Population figures showed a dramatic increase. In the Cape alone, the white population jumped from 182,000 in 1865 to 377,000 in 1891.

FINALLY, to crown all these discoveries, abundant cheap coal was found in 1887 along the Reef. It provided an economical source of power to run the gold-mining machinery and made possible a host of secondary industries which were started once there were railroads to transport their raw materials and markets for their products. A complete industrial revolution had begun which, though starting slowly, has continued with increasing momentum to the present day.

After World War II, this industrial revolution gained such startling force that South Africa for the past two decades has been one of the world's most favored countries economically. Different economists give different dates as the point from which this remarkable growth really began. Some pinpoint 1925, when the South African Government adopted policies of tariff protection which stimulated home manufacturing. Others specify 1928, when the country's fast-expanding iron and steel industry was founded. But most would agree that a decision taken in 1934 by President Franklin D. Roosevelt in the distant United States was particularly important. In his desperate fight against the Great Depression, Roosevelt that year raised the price of gold from $20.67 to $35 an ounce. Instantly the South African gold-mining industry, which had been lagging, shifted into high gear. Money poured into the country for mine development and further funds would soon arrive to speed the resulting expansion of all the country's industries.

A fresh impetus was provided by World War II. Virtually cut off from European manufactured goods, South African manufacturing companies expanded to fill the vacuum. Buttressing all this business growth was the country's vast mineral wealth. In addition to the gold and diamonds, rich veins of iron ore, manganese, asbestos, platinum, copper and other valuable minerals had been found under the sun-baked veld. To add to the country's good fortune, it was discovered, as the nuclear age dawned, that uranium oxide could be produced as a by-product of the gold-mining industry and could even be recovered from the huge yellow mine dumps—mounds of waste material left after the gold extraction process—which dot the entire Reef.

The export of this uranium, along with the discovery of new gold fields in the Orange Free State and the Transvaal, helped redouble the South African boom when the war ended. In the "gilt-edged years," as the period since World War II is sometimes called, industrial production increased more than five times, from about $850 million to well over $4.5 billion annually, and the country's gross national product shot up from approximately $2 billion to about $10 billion a year. Back in 1877, before gold had been discovered, the cash in the Transvaal treasury amounted at one moment to the paltry sum of only 12 shillings and sixpence (equal then to about three dollars).

Gold and diamonds remain vital to South Africa's whole economy. The soft yellow metal has remained in demand by the world's governments and banking systems. South Africa's gold reserves more than make up what might otherwise be a heavy yearly deficit in foreign exchange. In 1966 South Africa produced three quarters of the free world's gold. In addition, a glittering total of $74 million worth of South African diamonds was sold that year.

But gold and diamonds are only half the story of the country's remarkable economic expansion. The other half is, simply, huge profits. For a complex group of reasons, money invested in South African industry not infrequently returns an astounding 27 per cent a year. Low corporate taxes (compared with those in other modern nations) plus abundant raw materials and low wages (especially those paid to African workers) explain, in part, this extraordinary profit margin. In such circumstances, when an investor can hope to double his money in about three years, it is little wonder that a flood of new capital has poured into South Africa. A stock issue of a fish-processing company recently put on the market was oversubscribed 30 times. The $350 million needed to equip plants for the extraction of uranium oxide when that new industry sprang up in the early 1950s was raised with ease, largely in Britain and the United States.

THE RICH OPPENHEIMER DYNASTY

Successors to Rhodes and Barnato as the towering giants of South African finance have been the Oppenheimers, father and son. The father, Sir Ernest Oppenheimer, was born in Germany in 1880 and went to South Africa in 1902. He shortly engineered a coup which outfoxed the monopolistic De Beers diamond combine. Acquiring control of some gold mines as well as some diamond fields, he formed the Anglo American Corporation and by 1926 he was powerful enough to gain 50 per cent ownership of De Beers. He was also for many years a member of South Africa's Parliament. On his death in 1957, Sir Ernest's son, Harry Oppenheimer, succeeded to his father's empire. A careful businessman, Harry has nonetheless increased Anglo American's assets to the point where the company's total value is estimated at around $4,000 million.

As one of the last countries where the get-rich-quick dream can still be realized, South Africa also attracts managerial talent of the most daring stripe. Businessmen have made fortunes in a few years that elsewhere would take decades to amass. The standard of living of the nation's business managers—and even of sub-submanagers—is extraordinarily lavish. A successful Johannesburg businessman would no more do without a swimming pool and multiple automobiles than would a Hollywood star.

The South African economy must, however, put

up with built-in instability arising from the political situation. In the postwar years expansion has received only one check, but it was a serious one, and of a sort that might be repeated. This economic downturn began in 1958 when foreign investors, alarmed by the strong independence movements in the Congo, Kenya and the rest of Africa, began to withdraw capital from South Africa. The Sharpeville massacre of 1960, which seemed a harbinger of worse violence to come, turned the outflow of capital into a torrent. Some South African businessmen joined in the panic and began transferring their private fortunes to banks in England and Switzerland. Confidence had vanished overnight, and investors were in despair.

Finally, in 1961 the Government overcame its traditional reluctance to interfere in any way with business and imposed strict measures to halt the outflow of capital. Confidence returned, whereupon foreign investors once more began pouring money into the country. United States private investment in South Africa today is estimated at more than a billion dollars. Only a very timid investor refuses to gamble when he can expect a 27 per cent return on his money. Only a very unusual investor, furthermore, refuses to seek such profits because of his repugnance for such things as legalized racial discrimination and Nationalist Afrikaner racial policies in general. The temporary slowdown that began in 1958 did show, however, that South African prosperity must depend ultimately on the Government's ability to find ways of living harmoniously with black neighboring countries and of establishing racial peace at home.

YET even if, by force, racial peace is maintained, the South African economy faces another impasse which may slow or halt its expansion. This impasse is a shortage of skilled workers, a shortage which in the long run cannot be made good unless Africans are educated and trained for better jobs. It is just this sort of education and training that the South African Government seems set on denying to the black man. The automation of industry, the importation of skilled European workers and the wholesale circumventing of regulations have heretofore provided a partial solution to the problem, but these measures are now palpably failing to meet the needs of South Africa's rapidly expanding industrial society.

A far more serious aspect of South Africa's economy, from a human point of view, is the wage level of the African worker. One estimate of the per capita income of the white man in South Africa is $1,745 a year, of the African only $126 and of the Asian only slightly higher. In terms of week-to-week survival, this inequality of return for labor becomes even more dramatic. Recently, the manager of a clothing factory in Benoni, a town near Johannesburg, defended himself from a charge of underpaying his African help by boasting that, with overtime, his workers were making the munificent sum of $14 for a 55-hour week. This appears even less defensible in a country whose white population enjoys one of the world's highest standards of living.

IN fact, the whole South African industrial revolution has been for the African a bitter and grueling experience, just as the European Industrial Revolution was a bitter and grueling experience for the English working-classes in the early 19th Century. But the effect in both cases was the same—to precipitate into the modern world those who had hitherto either been living on its fringes or left outside it altogether. Since the discovery of gold and diamonds, millions of Africans have flocked to the cities, forsaking the localities associated with their ancestors and loosening their ties with their own past and their own people. Arriving in the cities, they have either lived in compounds, thousands of men herded into barracks without wives or womenfolk, or they have flocked into "locations" set apart for them beyond the suburbs, where their life has been not the immemorial life of Africa but a poor imitation of the life of whites. If, as South African Government propagandists claim, the black man in South Africa is better off financially and more advanced technically than most Africans elsewhere on the continent, he has yet to receive his due share of the wealth which his labor has so largely created.

Indeed, it can be argued that it is the black man's physical labor which has given the Afrikaner Nationalist Governments of the last decade and a half the financial resources and the power to carry out their racial policies. And these policies are designed in part to insure that the black man will *never* get his full share of South Africa's prosperity.

DIGGING A TUNNEL more than a mile down, African workers develop a new gold mine near Johannesburg. At this depth, water seeping into the mine must be pumped out constantly.

SORTING DIAMONDS, an expert at Consolidated House in Kimberley examines part of a week's yield from the De Beers mines, dividing it into categories based on quality, color and size.

An Empire Based upon Underground Treasures

The discovery of gold and diamonds in the 19th Century transformed South Africa from a thinly populated, agricultural backwater into a booming economic power. Today a few great corporations control the mining of precious metals in the country—a fabulously lucrative enterprise. De Beers Consolidated Mines not only controls the diamond industry but also markets three fourths of the world's production of natural diamonds. Similarly, gold mining is dominated by seven big financial houses. But the affluence of management stands in startling contrast to the poverty of African labor. Despite modern methods and good medical care, mining remains a dangerous occupation. More than 1,000 African miners die each year from accidents and disease, while working for an annual wage of about $200 cash plus maintenance.

A BIG REFINERY purifies rough gold, preparing it for sale on world markets

SHIMMERING PRODUCT at the Rand Refinery in Johannesburg *(right)* is stamped with serial numbers, with the company's hallmarks and with figures that indicate the percentage of pure gold. Almost all of the gold from South Africa's mines is refined here.

SKILLED WORKERS, who hold jobs forbidden to non-Europeans, pour molten gold *(opposite)* into a mold at the Rand Refinery. The refinery takes rough bullion, which is mixed with silver and base metals, and turns out gold bars at least 99.5 per cent pure.

LIQUID METAL pours into a mold *(below)*, where it will harden to become a bar weighing 400 ounces. In the refining process, the rough bars from the mines are melted, borax is added, and chlorine gas is passed through the liquid to produce pure gold.

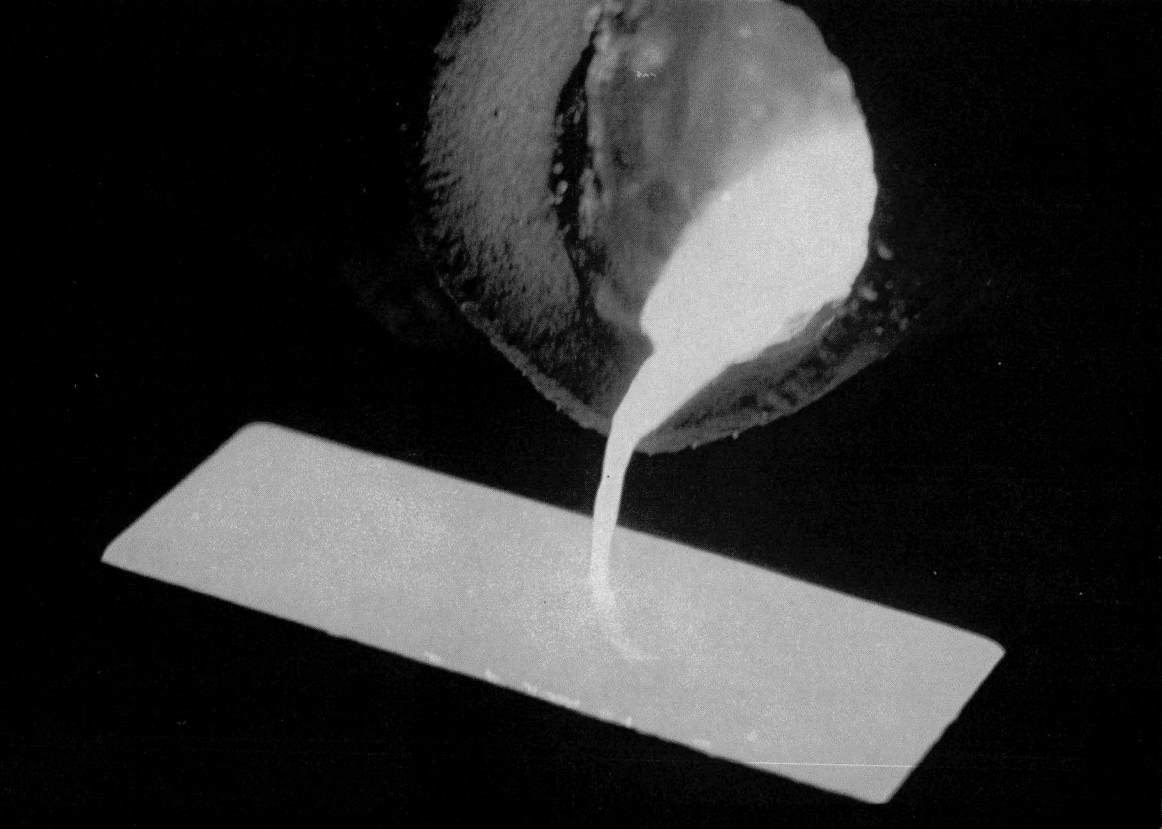

TOP LEADERS of the Anglo American Corporation of South Africa meet in the company offices in Johannesburg. Harry F. Oppenheimer *(right foreground)* dominates South African mining more than any other man. He is chairman of two interrelated firms—Anglo American and De Beers Consolidated Mines —which in turn have stakes in hundreds of other companies.

GIANT CORPORATIONS effectively control the nation's great mineral wealth

INDEPENDENT PROSPECTORS wait as a week's yield of diamonds is evaluated by a De Beers representative. Most prospectors are old, since licensing was all but stopped in 1935.

FRESH WORKERS sign in for their shift on a revolving drum at a De Beers diamond mine *(below)*. Diamond miners work for seven or nine months, then return to their tribal "homelands."

CROWDED QUARTERS, filled with concrete bunks, surround African miners who eat and talk during off-hours at Eastern Rand Proprietary Mines (E.R.P.M.), not far from Johannesburg.

UNIFORMED TRIBAL LEADERS at E.R.P.M., who are both counselors and policemen, advise fellow tribesmen. They hear miners' complaints, settle disputes and draft compound rules.

MINEWORKERS fresh from backward,

NEW RECRUITS undergo training as unskilled "trammers" *(left)*, learning to haul ore out of the mine in wheeled buckets, or trams. Such simple work requires only a few days' training.

impoverished tribal areas receive training in rudimentary tasks from a big company

LEADERSHIP TEST at Eastern Rand Proprietary Mines requires workers to carry a length of pipe across a pool. The complete series of tests poses problems of varying difficulty to a group of men without a leader. Whoever appears to put himself in charge of the group and thus shows leadership abilities may be promoted to "boss boy" and supervise other workers.

Accompanied by mounted units, British infantrymen during the Boer War cross a river near Kimberley by lifeline. Although the British

soon gained the upper hand, Boer guerrillas prolonged the conflict.

4

Open War between Boer and Briton

WITH the discovery of the major gold fields in the Transvaal in the 1880s, a clash began to threaten, a clash between Boer and Briton, farmer and financier, 18th Century and 19th. Actual war, however, might have been avoided, and the struggle fought out by other means, had not a new factor entered the situation. This new factor was the arrival in southern Africa of the Germans, who simultaneously barred the road north to the interior and threatened Britain's round-the-Cape routes to India and the East. A challenge of this magnitude to British trade and empire could not be ignored in London, and the British Government was drawn into what might otherwise have remained a local dispute.

The German appearance in Africa was dramatic, startling all of Europe. German traders and missionaries had long been active up and down the west coast between the Cape Colony and Angola, but the sandy wastes of this grimly named "Skeleton Coast" were generally held to be valueless, and the British had been content to annex what seemed the only serviceable harbor, Walvis Bay (Whale Bay), which is still a port for antarctic whalers. Now, in 1883, the Germans ran up their flag in Lüderitz Bay, 250 miles south of Walvis Bay, proclaimed the whole of South-West Africa a German protectorate and began to survey the route for a railroad to the east.

The danger was obvious. It would be easy for Germany to establish friendly relations with the Transvaal, where the pro-German Stephanus Johannes Paulus Kruger (known as *Oom Paul,* or Uncle Paul) had lately been elected President. A large part of the east coast, both north and south of Natal, was at this time unclaimed by any European nation. With a base in South-West Africa, and another in some as-yet-unclaimed part of the east coast, Germany could divide the continent. The Germans would thus cut off the British in South Africa from any chance of northward expansion, and so from realizing a vision which would increasingly grip the British imagination, that of a route from "the Cape to Cairo."

CECIL RHODES, who dreamed of an all-British Africa, was instrumental in securing large areas for the Crown, including the Rhodesias, which were named for him.

Britain moved decisively. Pondoland was made a British protectorate in 1885 and annexed in 1894, linking the Cape Colony with Natal and securing the whole eastern coastline up to Zululand. (Zululand itself was annexed to Natal in 1897.) Tongaland came after Pondoland. A small territory between Zululand and Portuguese East Africa, Tongaland was much coveted by Kruger since if its small port at Kosi Bay could be developed, the Transvaal would have its own outlet to the sea. The British had been prepared to let Kruger have his way. In January 1895, however, on the Kaiser's birthday, Kruger made a speech to the community of German immigrants in Pretoria, saying that German expansion in southern Africa should be encouraged to balance British power. The British had their ears open, and within three months Tongaland had been annexed and Kruger's republic cut off from its coveted outlet to the Indian Ocean.

Cooperating in all these moves, and spurring the British Government on to action during frequent visits to London, was the restless and dominating spirit of Cecil Rhodes. Rhodes was a visionary. His vision was of an "all-Red" Africa—red being the color used to identify British territory on maps of the world—an Africa united and at peace under British rule. He saw everything in life in terms of this imperial project. The Cape, which he ruled as Prime Minister from 1890 to 1896, was the base from which to operate. Diamonds and gold mines were there to give him the resources demanded by his far-ranging plans. His friends, his political allies, his business associates—all were tools to be employed in furthering his grand, ultimate design for Africa.

The next British move was made not on the east coast but in the center of southern Africa. Half of Bechuanaland was annexed in 1885, and a protectorate was established over the remaining half. The huge territory of Bechuanaland was, and is, largely desert, but it gave Rhodes what he wanted, control of "the bottleneck" between Kruger's Transvaal and the Germans in South-West Africa. It also secured the "Suez Canal northwards" route into what became the Rhodesias, the southwestern part of which was known as Matabeleland. Somewhere in this territory, Rhodes firmly believed, he would find a far greater Reef than the one already discovered—containing the fabulous "King Solomon's mines" from which had come the Biblical gold of Ophir. The money of investors and the support of powerful political interests would be drawn in behind Rhodes's British South Africa Company by the new discoveries of gold. Matabeleland would be annexed by Britain and, "If we get Matabeleland," Rhodes wrote, "we shall get the balance of Africa."

In 1889 Rhodes succeeded, after much intrigue and hard negotiation, in persuading the British Government to grant a Royal Charter to his company. Armed with this, and a still harder-won concession from Lobengula, ruler of the Matabele, Rhodes sent a "pioneer column"—in effect a small private army

—into Mashonaland, a territorial neighbor of Matabeleland directly north of the Transvaal.

By 1895, therefore, the whole map of southern Africa had changed. It was now no longer the British in South Africa who were cut off from expansion northwards; it was Kruger in the Transvaal who felt himself increasingly hemmed in by the British.

Paul Kruger, by now nearly 70 years old, was as remarkable a man in his own way as Cecil Rhodes. As a boy of 10 he had taken part in the Great Trek. Trekkers got little schooling, and Kruger had only three months of it, but what he lacked in education he made up for in native shrewdness. Asked once to apportion an estate between two brothers who were quarreling, he said: "Let one brother divide the land, and the other take first choice."

PAUL KRUGER, Rhodes's great antagonist, personified Boer resistance to British aims. Kruger was the Transvaal's President from 1883 until 1900, but died in exile.

While still a young man, Kruger was converted to the Dopper Church, the most extreme of the Afrikaner Calvinist sects. It has been said that he regarded hymn singing as "wicked levity," but this is not quite the case. To sing hymns at home or on the veld need incur no censure. What was clearly inexcusable was to sing them in church, since they formed no part of Holy Writ. The Bible was Kruger's constant companion, and since it contained for him the answer to every political, military or scientific problem, he read nothing else.

A farmer by vocation, Kruger had also served in the commandos, his people's militia. Each commando (originally a Portuguese word) enrolled all able-bodied white men over 16 in its district, elected its own officers and was subject to call at any time. Kruger began as a field cornet in a local commando, rising eventually to the office of Commandant General of the entire Transvaal. Though he was rocklike in determination, his influence was consistently on the side of moderation and the upholding of law and order. He was not without a dour sense of humor. Like Rhodes, he was ambitious and had a vision—the vision of a united Boer republic governing all of South Africa. Clearly the two visions were in conflict. "I pity the man," said Rhodes of Kruger. ". . . . When I see a man starting and continuing with one object, and utterly failing in that object, I cannot help pitying him."

"This man was the curse of Africa," was what Kruger said of Rhodes. Both statements were grave errors of judgment. In 1895, however, it did indeed seem that Kruger's plans had failed and that his republic was cut off from hope of expansion. Moreover, he had good reason to fear Britain's next move.

Not many years before, in 1877, at a time when the Transvaal was divided by poverty and weak administration and was almost bankrupt, Theophilus Shepstone, Britain's Secretary for Native Affairs in Natal, had gone to Pretoria with 25 police to annex the Transvaal. The attempt was part of a wider plan to unite the various territories of South Africa into a federation. The federation project had some Boer backing, and for the moment the annexation passed unchallenged. But almost four years later the Boers rose in what is sometimes known as the First Boer War, defeated the British at Majuba Hill, and regained their independence. The plan for bringing the Transvaal into a federation, however, had never been abandoned, as Kruger knew, and now the combination of imperial interests with financial ones, personified in the financier-imperialist Cecil Rhodes, could well bring a second attempt to annex the Transvaal and unify South Africa under British rule.

The discovery of gold on the Reef, Rhodes had said, was "the biggest thing the world has seen." But Kruger and his Boers looked on the discovery of gold as a disaster, and the crowd of get-rich-quicks who came flooding into the country in the late 1880s and 1890s was simply the same British (in a far worse form) from whom, for over half a century, the Boers had been trying to escape. The Boers called these English interlopers *Uitlanders* (foreigners). By 1895 there were 80,000 "foreigners" in the Transvaal, outnumbering the Boers by more than two to one. "They have grown fat on my land," Kruger complained. "Every ounce of gold taken from the bowels of our soil," he foretold grimly, "will yet have to be weighed up with rivers of tears." Kruger hated Johannesburg, the center of *Uitlander* development. Though he lived little more than 30 miles away, in Pretoria, he went to Johannesburg only three times in the course of his life. Called upon to speak during one of his rare visits, he began: "Burghers, friends, murderers, thieves and robbers. . . ."

SLOWLY Boer resentment was crystallizing. So was that of the despised *Uitlanders*. The chief grievance of the "foreigners" was that although they had so great a stake in the Transvaal, being responsible for perhaps nine tenths of its revenues, the Transvaal Government, led by Kruger, denied them the vote.

According to Lionel Phillips, an *Uitlander* who was an important figure in the mining industry, many people did not care "a fig for the franchise." But they did want some means of electing representatives who could remedy their grievances. And now that possibility was being made more and more remote. Before 1882 an immigrant needed to reside in the Transvaal only 12 months to acquire the full franchise. Later this was raised to five years. In 1890 the qualifying period was lengthened to 14 years—with every likelihood that, if it ever appeared many *Uitlanders* would qualify, the period would be lengthened again. "Make friends of your *Uitlanders*," had been the advice of the wise old President of the Orange Free State, Jan Hendrik Brand. "I will never give them anything," was Kruger's response. Public petitions were scorned, and one member of the Volksraad, or Parliament, challenged the *Uitlanders*, if they wanted the vote, to fight for it.

The *Uitlanders* suffered other grievances of a practical kind. Kruger wanted a railroad to Delagoa Bay, so as to have an outlet through Portuguese rather than British territory, and for a time he refused to allow railroads from Natal and the Cape to be extended into the Transvaal, thus needlessly raising the cost of many commodities. Besides taxing the mines heavily, the Pretoria Government sold concessions to favored people, giving them monopolies of certain supplies necessary for working the mines. The dynamite monopoly drove up the price of explosives to three times their normal cost, adding three million dollars a year to the mining companies' expenses. There was also extreme governmental inefficiency. The rudimentary administrative setup in Pretoria, which had served well enough for a pastoral republic, was lost in trying to control the workings of a rapidly expanding industrial state. It took two years, for example, to decide the scale of cab fares for Johannesburg. The only remedies for harassed businessmen were personal visits to the responsible officials—often reinforced with a bribe.

When the political highroad is barred, men try the path of conspiracy. The National Union had been formed in 1892 under the leadership of English-speaking South Africans to present the *Uitlanders'* grievances to Kruger's Government. When all the Union's demands were rejected by Kruger, the Union began to work for his Government's overthrow. With the backing of Rhodes in the Cape, arms were smuggled into Johannesburg hidden in coal trucks and concealed inside oil drums.

IN the last days of December 1895, the plotting reached its climax. There was to be a rising in Johannesburg, and simultaneously a column of volunteers and police from Rhodes's British South Africa Company was to advance on the city from the Bechuanaland border, under the command of Rhodes's henchman, Dr. Leander Starr Jameson. The projected rising, however, was far too generally known. The population of Johannesburg panicked, and at the last moment the leaders of the plot within the city, divided in their intentions, tried to call off the whole attempt. But by then the only thing which would have held Jameson back was a categorical stop order from Rhodes—which was not sent.

Jameson started out. At Krugersdorp, 20 miles west of Johannesburg, his force was easily surrounded by Boer commandos. Jameson's troops were taken prisoner to Pretoria, and the leaders of the plot handed over to the British Government for trial. Kruger's Government behaved throughout with dignity, humanity and common sense. So ended the ill-conceived "Jameson Raid." But its lamentable consequences were still to come. Rhodes's complicity in a plot to overthrow the Boer republic cut short instantly the cooperation he had received from such moderate Afrikaner politicians as Jan Hofmeyr and W. P. Schreiner, who with Rhodes had controlled political life in the Cape Colony for the past five years, an alliance which might have transformed for the better the whole future of South African political life. Rhodes, discredited, had no choice but to resign as Prime Minister.

The folly of the raid, Hofmeyr said, "threw back the cause of civilization in South Africa for 25 years." If it had been only for 25 years, the price would have been small. And though it was Kruger's intransigence—based on his fear of being outvoted and so losing domination—which inflamed the ill-feeling between the English-speaking people and the Afrikaners, it was Rhodes's double-dealing which aborted all hope of a peaceful solution.

In the years following the Jameson Raid the Boers began stockpiling arms and ammunition in the Transvaal and a new figure loomed in South African politics: Sir Alfred Milner, the new British High Commissioner in the Cape Colony, who was to play an important role in South Africa after the Boer War. Moderate Afrikaners—including some who had vainly cooperated with Rhodes—brought Milner and Kruger together in June 1899 to discuss the *Uitlander* franchise. The conference ended in failure.

British public opinion against the Boers mounted, stirred by thoughts of Empire and by the infringement of Uitlander rights. In September, Kruger began mobilizing troops in the Transvaal. He then put forward an ultimatum asserting that the franchise issue was the business of the Transvaal alone and demanding the removal of recently arrived British troops. The British rejected his ultimatum on October 11, 1899, and the next day the Boers invaded the Cape Colony from the Transvaal.

THE advantage for the moment lay with the Boers, who outnumbered the 25,000 British troops in the country by two to one, and whose commandos were able to mobilize rapidly. But Britain had ordered reinforcements from India and the Mediterranean as well as from the home country, so that it was essential for the Boers to achieve a quick decision before the Empire's force could be brought to bear. To do this they had to arouse, by rapid moves

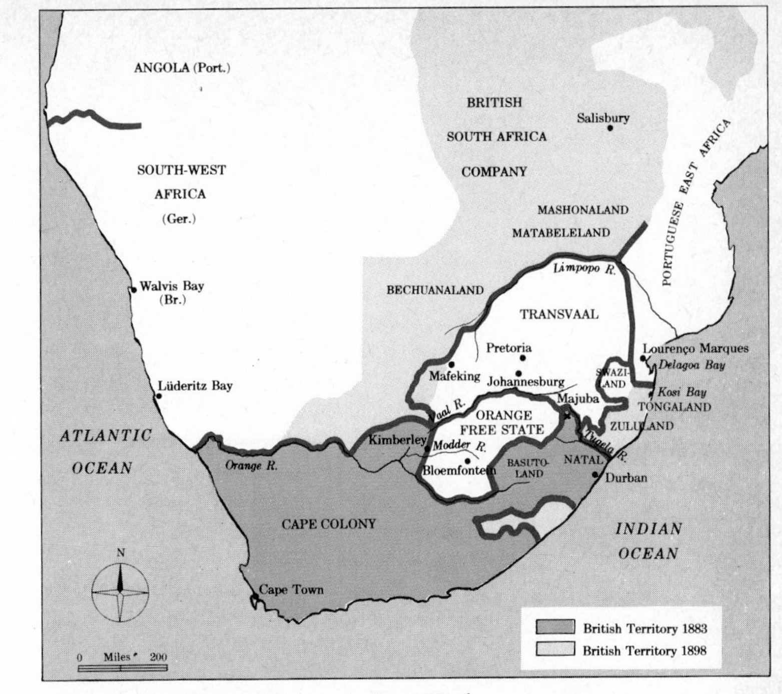

STRATEGIC MOVES leading to the Boer War began in 1883, when Germany claimed the coastal region of South-West Africa. Though borders were vague, the Cape British feared the Germans would link up with the Transvaal Boers and isolate them. By 1898 the Boers had taken Swaziland, but the British had annexed far more territory, and now the Boers felt encircled.

southwards, the Afrikaners in the Cape to rebel against the British Government there; at the same time they needed to seize Durban on their flank.

But the Boers lacked a unified command, and their generals, including Commandant General Piet Joubert and the popular Piet Cronje, made the mistake of becoming involved in three sieges—those of Ladysmith in Natal, Kimberley in the Orange Free State and Mafeking, on the border of the Cape and the Transvaal. These sieges tied down their forces, robbing them of their great advantage, mobility.

Fortunately for the Boers, they had another advantage—the character of the British Commander, Sir Redvers Buller, who combined obstinacy with hesitation to a remarkable degree. As reinforcements—an entire fresh Army corps of 48,800 men—began to land at the Cape, Buller divided them into three uneven columns instead of smashing the Boers with a concentrated force. None of the columns was powerful enough in itself, and during "Black Week," December 9-15, 1899, all three were decisively defeated. General Lord Methuen, advancing from the Orange River with some 9,000 men to relieve Kimberley, sustained almost 900 casualties fighting three engagements along the route. And then a large Boer force—which Methuen later claimed had numbered 16,000—attacked and brought down another 948 men in the Battle of Magersfontein. Having lost more than 20 per cent of his column, Methuen was forced to withdraw to the Modder River.

A second column of 3,000 men, led by General Sir William Gatacre, suffered lighter casualties but was also defeated. Gatacre's men were turned back by troops from the Orange Free State at Stormberg with the loss of 600 prisoners and more than 100 killed and wounded. General Buller himself, advancing on the right into Natal with 21,000 men, was defeated at Colenso, south of Ladysmith, losing 1,100 men in a disastrous battle.

These disasters roused a prompt reaction in Britain. Field Marshal Lord Roberts, who had served more than 40 years in India, was brought in as Commander in Chief, superseding Buller. Major General Lord Kitchener, who had become a British national hero with his victories in the Sudan, was to be Roberts' Chief of Staff. Reinforcements would include contingents from Canada and Australia.

Roberts moved fast. By the end of February 1900, less than three months after Black Week, he had relieved Kimberley and rounded up General Cronje with 4,000 of his men at Paardeberg. On March 13 Roberts entered Bloemfontein, the capital of the Orange Free State. The Orange Free State troops who were helping to besiege Ladysmith thereupon came home to protect their families and farms. Ladysmith was soon relieved, and all of Natal was abandoned by the Boers.

AFTER these dramatic successes the British were forced to pause. Enteric fever laid low many of the troops. Supplies and ammunition had to be brought over the veld from the Cape by oxcart. But in May, when Roberts struck again, he quickly took Johannesburg and the Transvaal capital, Pretoria. On September 1 the Transvaal was annexed by Britain, and 10 days later Paul Kruger, aged and broken, slipped across the border into Portuguese East Africa. From there he left for Europe on a Dutch warship. Less than a year after the beginning of the war, Roberts—with most others—believed it was already over. Many Boer soldiers, discouraged, had gone home to their farms. Roberts himself left Cape Town for England in December 1900. But as it turned out, the war was entering its longest and bitterest phase, one which would have fateful consequences for relations between the two white groups.

Of the original Boer commanders, Joubert had died and Cronje was a British prisoner. They were succeeded, however, by much abler men, the energetic and determined Louis Botha and two brilliant leaders of guerrillas, Christian de Wet and Jacobus de la Rey. These men settled on a new strategy whose success soon drew back into the field many of the burghers who had given up and gone home. From now on the Boers avoided pitched battles and fell back on guerrilla tactics. They used their superior knowledge of the country and great mobility to make lightning raids, particularly on railroads and supplies. Every farmhouse became a potential base where guerrillas could hide and from which they could organize attacks. The British replied by constructing blockhouses along the railroads and by burning any farmhouse from which shots were fired.

REFUGEES, particularly women and children from the destroyed farms, were rounded up into concentration camps by the British. The purpose of these camps was to protect the homeless, but through ignorance and lack of resources, the camps were inadequately supervised, and out of 150,000 inmates 26,000 died. Their deaths were due to disease and to inadequate knowledge of hygiene. In Boer tradition, however, these deaths are ascribed to British cruelty. The camp guards, so one obscure legend has it, forced the inmates to eat "fungus" —i.e., mushrooms—which for some reason were thought to have had fatal effects. The British are also supposed to have mixed ground glass in the inmates' oatmeal. A bowl of this malign concoction is believed by many Afrikaners still to exist—damning evidence of British inhumanity. A lasting tragedy, the fate of these 26,000 dead still deeply embitters relations between the peoples. From the point of view of British military policy, the camps were a costly mistake, since the women and children were cared for while their men continued to fight.

Under these conditions the war dragged on for a further 18 months, and it was not until May 31, 1902, that a peace treaty—the Treaty of Vereeniging

—was signed. When it came it was a generous one. Its terms included $14.4 million to be paid by the British for repairing farm damage, and loans, free of interest for two years, for resettling farmers on their land. It also called for a British-run Government to administer the Transvaal and the Orange Free State. The Governor of the two former Boer republics was Alfred Milner, now Lord Milner. Tactless and self-opinionated, but with great capacity and drive, he soon established an administration which was enlightened, impartial and respected.

BACK in England, however, the provisions of the treaty were deemed harsh by the new Liberal Government which won the British election of 1906. The Liberals had always opposed the Boer War, and under their rule Lord Milner was soon relieved and the Transvaal and Orange Free State given partial self-government. This move was followed by the calling of a South African National Convention, which drafted an Act of Union—enacted by the British Parliament just eight years after the peace treaty was signed—whereby the four territories, Cape Colony, Natal, the Orange Free State and the Transvaal, were combined into the Union of South Africa. Federation, which so many South Africans had dreamed of for so long, was now a fact.

The new Union, coming so soon after a bitter conflict, was hailed as a great act of statesmanship which would bring Boer and Briton together and inaugurate a golden age of cooperation between the peoples. "The Constitution is not a man's work," declared General Jan Christian Smuts. "It bears the impress of a Higher Hand." Smuts, who had been an outstanding Boer commander, was now second in the Transvaal only to General Louis Botha, who had become its Prime Minister. Jan Hofmeyr, nephew and namesake of the great politician of Rhodes's day, wrote in his history of South Africa: "Five years after the Peace of Vereeniging had ended the career of the two Republics, those same territories were ruled as British Colonies by the defeated generals who had signed that Peace. The . . . [British] Government had embarked upon a magnificent venture of faith."

What Smuts and Hofmeyr had in mind was the fact that since Boers heavily outnumbered British over the four territories, the British were voluntarily placing their future in the hands of their former enemies. Smuts and Botha always remembered this; they regarded it as a sacred trust to ensure that English-speaking South Africans should not suffer for their act of faith. Some later Afrikaner politicians, however, would regard the act of faith simply as an act of folly which delivered the English-speaking enemy into their hands.

The Africans, for their part, today view this act of faith as an act of betrayal. At the time of the war and the subsequent Act of Union, Africans enjoyed the vote in the Cape Colony on equal terms with whites. In the Transvaal and the Free State they were voteless, and they were almost voteless in Natal, but it was thought likely that Natal in the course of time would follow the Cape's more liberal pattern. At the Convention which framed the Act of Union, all the Cape delegates—Afrikaners and English-speaking alike—fought for the common franchise. The delegates from the Transvaal and the Orange Free State opposed it tooth and nail. Finally, a compromise was reached leaving matters largely as they were but safeguarding the Cape franchise by entrenching it in a clause of the Constitution.

THERE is no doubt that, in accepting the compromise, the Cape delegates believed that time was on their side and that, with the natural spread of tolerance and an increasing belief in the value of human rights throughout the world, South Africa too would be affected and the franchise extended by degrees to all, regardless of color. In fact, it has been the intolerance of the Transvaal and the Free State which has spread to cover Natal and the Cape. A constitutional amendment in 1936 removed Africans in the Cape from the common voting roll there, and since the Nationalists came to power in the late 1940s, ways have been found to deprive all Africans and Coloreds of their voting rights.

The calculation that the two white groups would soon be welded together in amity proved wrong as well. Today, though there is a measure of political agreement, humanly and socially the Afrikaner and the English-speaking South African are little closer than they were, and nowhere near so close as men of goodwill in both camps predicted they would be.

GOLD PROSPECTORS and the African workers gather around claim near Barberton in the Tran vaal in the 1880s. Thousands c fortune-seekers came to the Tran vaal, most of them heading for th Witwatersrand gold fields. Soo they outnumbered the Boers, an open hostility quickly develope

A MAZE OF CABLES stretches above the Kimberley diamond mine during the years when individual diggers worked their own square claims. Before the claims were amalgamated in 1888, each prospector relayed ore in buckets along his cable to helpers at the edge of the pit.

A Scramble That Brought On a War

From their first confrontation in South Africa, a strong antipathy often arose between Boer and Briton, and the discovery of gold and diamonds in the late 19th Century aggravated the situation. A flood of foreigners, mostly English-speaking, came to seek their fortunes in mining; when their demands for political rights in the Boer republic of the Transvaal were repeatedly denied, the resulting tensions helped to provoke the Boer War (1899-1902). The British forces were superior to the Boers in numbers and organization, but only after a long and bitter struggle did they bring about the Boers' defeat. After the war the British created the Union of South Africa, and the two white groups were united under one government. But differing viewpoints and lingering resentment over the war still mar their relations today.

BOOM TOWN of Kimberley in 1888 *(below)* swarms with ox-drawn carts, horses and a horde of diamond miners. Besides the diggers who arrived from all over the world, gamblers, merchants, speculators and saloon-keepers came in droves, seeking to make a quick fortune.

CAPTURED GENERAL, the patriarchal Boer leader Piet Cronje (in broad-brimmed hat) was forced to surrender with 4,000 men to British forces on February 27, 1900. During the following months the British seized the Orange Free State and the Transvaal. However, Boer guerrillas continued the fight for two years more.

CONVALESCING OFFICERS sit in the sun at an unusually well-staffed and well-supplied British base hospital outside of Cape Town *(opposite)*. Two thirds of the 22,000 British and colonial soldiers who died in the war were victims of disease. In the spring of 1900, thousands of British troops were hospitalized with typhoid.

THE BOER WAR drew Britain and the Boer republics into three years of bitter conflict

BOER COMMANDOS man the trenches outside Mafeking *(opposite)*, where they held down a British garrison for more than seven months in 1899-1900. This and two other sieges undertaken by the Boers were strategic mistakes, for the delay gave the British time to land reinforcements.

BRITISH ASSAULT begins *(right)* as Canadian troops storm a hill held by Boer commandos in 1900. The British and colonial forces, used to open battle, found the Boers's elusiveness bewildering. After 1900 the Boers relied on guerrilla tactics, benefiting by their familiarity with the terrain.

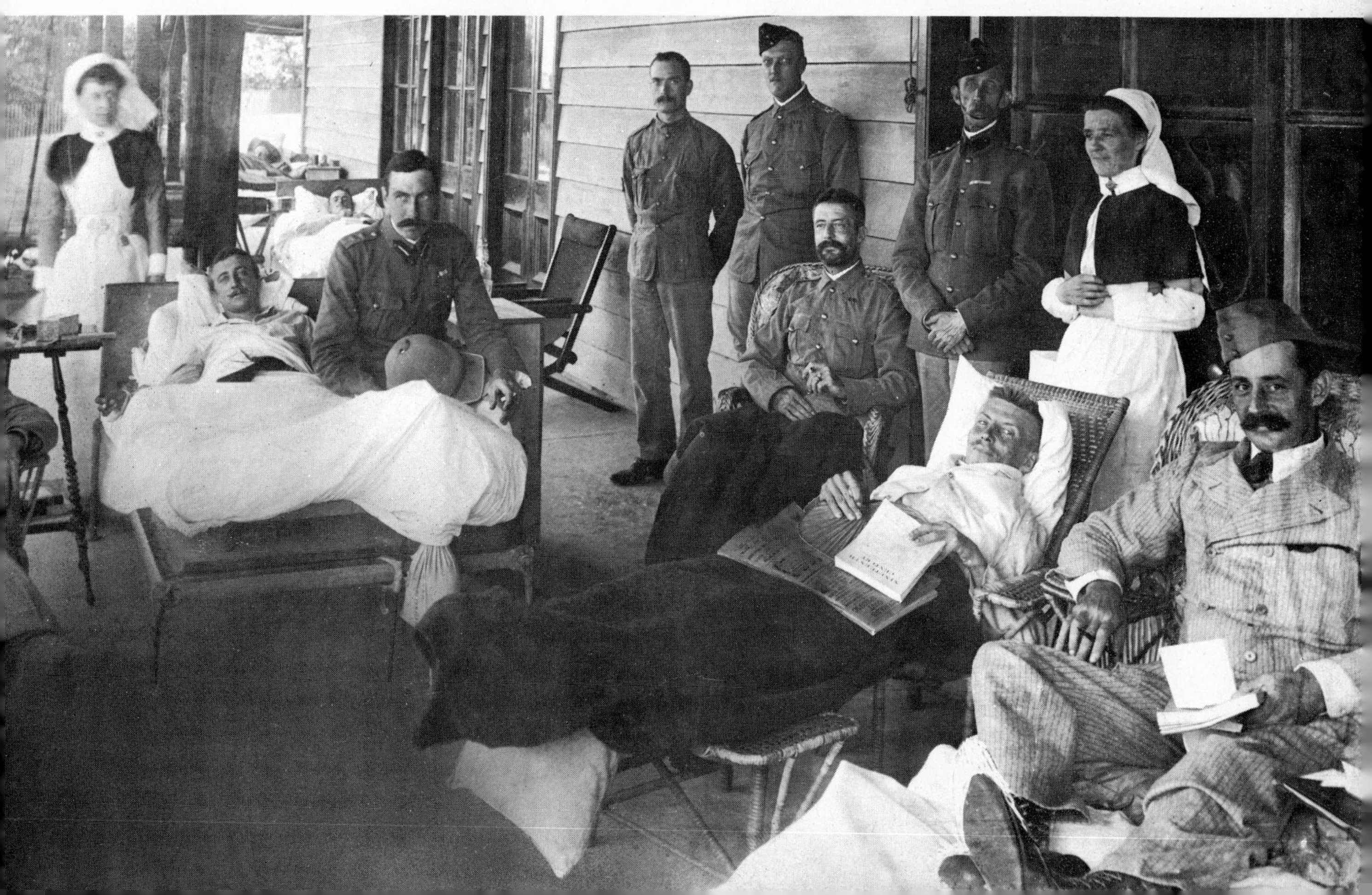

G.C.C.
4

A BRITISH LOOK is preserved in sports by the English-speaking

FASHIONABLE CROWD follows the races at the South African Turf Club's course in Kenilworth, near Cape Town. As in England, racing is a major social event.

WN BOWLING near Cape Town ab- rbs English-speaking men and women essed in club uniforms *(opposite)*, as bath- s in the distance bask on an ocean beach.

WINNING HORSE is led past the stands after a race at the Kenilworth track. Breeding race horses is a prestige hobby among the prosperous English-speaking whites.

A COUNTRY TOWN, Richmond is a white settlement with a separate African township *(background)* on the Cape Province plateau known as the Great Karroo. The Dutch Reformed church, its spire visible for miles, dominates the landscape.

The Privileged Life of the Whites

AFTER the Act of Union was passed in 1909, the English-speaking people of South Africa appear to have thought: "Well, that's that. The Afrikaner will inevitably dominate political life. But we've met him more than halfway, and by the time he's fully in power, he will have come the rest of the way to meet us. We've chosen a Boer general as Prime Minister—what more could we do to show our good faith? And now let's get on with what we came here for—making money and enjoying life."

Over the last 75 years the English-speaking people have made a great deal of money and have created a way of life almost unrivaled for comfort and convenience. The English-speaking tend to live in Natal, which was first settled by the British; on big farms in the eastern part of the Cape Province; or in the wealthier suburbs around Johannesburg, Cape Town, East London, Pretoria and Port Elizabeth. Big, airy houses in a profusion of styles, from Cape Dutch to the most modern, stand in large, shady gardens tended by one or more African gardeners. Swimming pools and tennis courts are the rule; looking down from the air as one comes into Johannesburg over the northern suburbs, one sees hardly a house without its own patch of blue water.

Offices begin work early in the morning, so that most businessmen are home by five or shortly after. Then starts the pleasant round of sport and social life. Golf and tennis are favorite sports of the prosperous, with horse racing on the weekends. A high proportion of families has a car for each parent and another for the children of university age. Rich farmers and mining magnates own private planes. Cocktail, bridge and dinner parties are the accepted forms of entertainment, and a ceaseless round of them goes on throughout the year.

A WELL-TO-DO household may have a staff of four or five servants: a houseboy, who waits on table in a white uniform with a red or green sash and white cotton gloves; a cook; a nursemaid if there are small children; a gardener or two; and perhaps a chauffeur. Poorer families or apartment-dwellers are content with a maid and a houseboy. Although recent legislation is tending to cut down numbers of domestic servants in the interests of industry, a white family would have to be nearly penniless before it tried to get along with no domestic help at all.

At 5 o'clock some cities, such as Johannesburg, become empty of whites as the rush out to the suburbs begins. On weekends, the suburbs in their turn see an exodus as the wealthier families pour out to their farms and coastal bungalows and the less wealthy content themselves with a day's drive to the mountains or go fishing and sailing on a bay.

For the English-speaking people who live in towns or cities, a favorite pastime—particularly for the middleaged—is the English game of bowls. Thousands spend the best part of every weekend on the bowling green—and a strangely old-fashioned appearance they present. Portly men in white flannel trousers and striped or brightly colored blazers, wearing Panama hats decorated with their club colors, carry little oddly shaped handbags which contain their favorite "woods" (bowling balls) to their local bowling greens. The women wear white flannel "costumes" —long skirts with either jackets or blazers, heavy brogues and broad-brimmed schoolgirl hats. An atmosphere of ritual and formality surrounds the game, and there is little sound except the occasional clack of bowling balls or a clatter from the clubhouse as the African servants wash the teacups.

Historically, the people of British origin came out to South Africa not by shiploads, as they went to Canada or the United States, but in handfuls or as individuals. Until the discovery of gold in the 1880s the white population was overwhelmingly Afrikaner. Many Britons came out then to seek wealth in the gold and diamond mines, but it was not until after World War II that a large-scale attempt was made to attract immigrants, and this program was closed down by the Nationalists in 1948 for fear the influx from overseas might reverse their precarious electoral lead. Only in the last few years has the door been reopened, Afrikaner fear of the English-speaking being outweighed by their fear of the overwhelming, and continuously increasing, black majority.

Those Britons who came out as individuals were mainly professional men or people with some mercantile experience. They came as doctors, lawyers, schoolmasters, engineers, merchants. To a lesser extent, they were skilled craftsmen—stonemasons, wheelwrights, wagon builders. A number of miners from Cornwall came out to the gold fields, but there was never a big working-class immigration.

AN important consequence of this fact that British immigrants tended to have education and professional skills or experience in business has been that English-speaking South Africans have founded, and still largely control, most of the country's industrial and commercial enterprises. Their contribution to the life of the country has been impressive. They are not only largely responsible for South Africa's mining and industrial development but also for the establishment of many of its towns and cities, ports and harbors, and for building much of the country's magnificent network of railroads and highways. It is mainly due to the English-speaking section—including South Africa's more than 100,000 Jews—that the country has developed in three quarters of a century from a backward agricultural community to a rich, semi-industrialized modern state.

In the field of education, the English-speaking people have been responsible for founding schools, universities and libraries. On the political side, they have fostered parliamentary institutions, the rule of law, the independence of the judiciary, the freedom of the press and many schemes of social welfare. The fact, so surprising to visitors, that a large part of the South African press continuously and boldly criticizes Government policies, is a legacy of British press freedom, stoutly defended by a handful of English-speaking editors and journalists.

Impressive as this contribution sounds, it has been vitiated by two tragic failures: the failure to extend their own heritage of democratic rights and institutions to include the nonwhite peoples, and the failure to establish terms of harmony and goodwill with the Afrikaners.

It must be conceded in its defense that the English-speaking minority has had only one long spell of political power since the country was united in 1909. This was the eight and a half years between September 1939 and May 1948 when Jan Christian Smuts was the Prime Minister and the largely English-speaking United Party had a majority in Parliament. Six of these were war years, however, and the remaining three were beset with postwar problems and grave shortages. With attention focused on the difficulties of war and its aftermath, the United Party somehow let slip its opportunity to carry through any program of electoral reform and social reconstruction.

Worse, in the years since 1948, during which the Nationalists have been passing a succession of restrictive laws, the English-speaking have only rarely offered serious and united resistance. Never at any time, despite their homeland's long tradition of liberty and democracy, have they come out openly for the extension of full democratic rights to the nonwhite peoples.

In general, the struggle has been left to a handful of so-called "liberals" and "progressives," whom the United Party has opposed and derided only slightly less bitterly than have the Nationalist Afrikaners. And although the members of the United Party would not themselves have initiated the Nationalists' most cruelly repressive measures, in time of crisis, such as followed the Sharpeville massacre in 1960, the Government has only to ask for emergency powers and they will be voted by the United Party members of Parliament with pledges of enthusiastic co-operation.

It is true that, being more responsive to the currents of world opinion, the English-speaking South Africans are less illiberal than the Afrikaners. Consequently, if they were in power today, they would make concessions to the needs and demands of the Africans which the Nationalist Government refuses. But this is a matter only of degree. The position can be stated in a nutshell: the majority of English-speaking and Afrikaners alike support a general apartheid. The difference between them is, first, in the way apartheid would be applied; and second, of tenacity, in that the English-speaking would give way when the pressure became too strong.

But if the English-speaking people have failed to share their heritage with the African, they have equally failed to reach real understanding with the Afrikaner. Confident, at least until 1948, that they could control the political situation through the exercise of their economic power, the English-speaking never went out of their way to establish ties of friendship with the Afrikaners through which some modifying influence might conceivably have been brought to bear. Today, although the two white peoples meet regularly in the pursuit of their business or professions, their social lives are spent apart. Veiled hostility at times becomes open—as in the attacks by Afrikaner students on English students demonstrating against apartheid.

This division is, perhaps, not strange, since the two groups show fundamentally different attitudes toward South Africa. The aim of the Afrikaner Nationalists is group domination in every field through the exercise of their political power. The aim of the

A QUEST FOR WHITE IMMIGRANTS

Since 1960 the South African Government has eagerly sought to attract white immigrants, especially skilled workers and men with managerial experience. Immigration offices have been set up in England, Holland, West Germany, Italy and Switzerland, and embassies and consulates elsewhere have been briefed to handle prospective immigrants. Full-page advertisements appear in European newspapers extolling the life in South Africa—the high wage levels of white workers, the climate, the inexpensive household help. The Government contributes $144 toward the passage of every immigrant and provides free accommodations for new arrivals until suitable employment is found. The Department of Immigration makes little secret of its preference for northern Europeans, but a recent influx of Italians and Portuguese has also met with a warm welcome. The entire program of attracting white immigrants seems to be successful: 48,000 arrived during 1966, about three times the 1961 figure and a big gain over 1960, when more people left the country than entered it.

English-speaking is a secure and agreeable life in a beautiful country. To the Afrikaner, South Africa is home, the only one he has, and he is passionately engaged in protecting this home from what he conceives to be forces that menace it. To some of the English-speaking, "home" still tends to mean England. If some Afrikaners exaggerate this tendency among the English-speaking, it is nonetheless true that should conditions in the Republic become intolerable, they count on being able to return to Britain or make a new home in some part of the Commonwealth, such as Australia or Canada. The Afrikaners, on the other hand, feel completely cut off from their ancestral homelands—generally the Netherlands or France. This was especially evident during World War II, when the English-speaking passionately supported the Allied cause while many Afrikaners, despite the fact that Holland and France were overrun by the Nazis, remained strongly pro-German.

Political observers have pointed out that the Afrikaners in South Africa and the Jews in Israel are the only peoples who feel that they have, in modern times, *created* their nations. And the two peoples, these observers go on to say, have several striking traits in common—a fierce nationalism, a tendency to reject all criticism as the work of schemers or fools, and a willingness to resort to arms in times of crisis. Many English-speaking South Africans, on the other hand, retain to some degree the old British colonial outlook—they remain "sojourners in the land."

THE fundamental criticism of the South Africans of British origin is that they are a halfhearted people who have never formulated in their own minds what it is they stand for, and for what—if anything—they would be prepared to fight. They know, in a vague way, what they would *like*. What they would like is to arrive at a general compromise on points of disagreement with the Afrikaners. They would like a slow liberalization of policy toward the African. They would like South Africa to become a respected, as well as a wealthy, part of the Western world instead of being—as it was called by the Nationalist newspaper *Die Burger*—the world's "polecat." They would like these things, but they would not fight for them. Many of them are even unwilling to devote the time and energy to political organization that would enable them to battle effectively for their views in Parliament. Their political methods are lax as their views are tepid; they are content to play golf three times a week and read the stockmarket reports.

Indecisive, halfhearted and lacking a definite policy of their own, the English-speaking are being increasingly drawn into supporting the Afrikaners' suppressive racial policies. But unlike most Afrikaners, the English-speaking are nagged by the suspicion that these policies will not succeed. And they believe that if apartheid fails, the white man, whatever his background and language, will be driven violently out of South Africa or else penned into a corner. The more thoughtful among the English-speaking also fear that when the upheaval comes, not only will they lose their businesses and their easy life but also, having helped bring this destiny upon themselves—with its repercussions upon Africa and perhaps upon all mankind—they may be far from welcome elsewhere in the world.

THE Afrikaner, in contrast to the English-speaking South African, is less likely to be an industrialist or merchant than a farmer or small tradesman, or even the foreman of a gang of laborers. The white proletariat is overwhelmingly Afrikaner, as anyone can see who attends a big rugby match or similar popular gathering. But if they are, to some extent, underdogs in the worlds of industry and finance, the Afrikaners are now top dogs in politics and are determined to have their own way in that sphere and to exploit their political supremacy to achieve power in other fields. They are also sustained and given unity—and even the sense of a glorious destiny—by their past, which to them is full of heroic victories over unbelievable hardships and perils.

The Afrikaner rides into history as a picturesque and self-sufficient pioneer, homely, hospitable and pious, opening up southern Africa with his gun, his Bible, his team of oxen and the great lumbering wagon which carried his wife and children, his simple farming equipment and all his other worldly goods. The wagon was his shelter, his transport, his fort against enemy attack. It is true, of course, that in the fertile valleys close to Cape Town, thousands of Boer families have lived a comfortable, settled life in the European style with never a thought of packing up and trekking into the interior. But they form no part of the great Afrikaner myth, which is dominated by the figure of the pioneer and his ox wagon. The life to which the Afrikaner people look back as to a golden age, the life around which center their books and pageants, plays and poems, is the life of the trekboer.

In the words of Sheila Patterson, who tells the story of the Afrikaner in *The Last Trek,* it was "a life when land was there for the taking, where the veld grass grew tall, where the fountains never failed and the game thundered in uncounted herds. A life where men were strong and God-fearing, their women fair and brave and where the Kaffir knew his place. A life where the Boers could be left to themselves, to live in quiet, free and exempt from taxation."

Other elements fill out the image the Afrikaner cherishes of his simple and heroic forebears. The trekboer families were large, and the father wielded undisputed authority. The mother was the center of the household and possessed all the virtues and skills of the frontier wife. Family ties were maintained with even the remotest cousins. Hospitality was generous and unfailing so that the traveler—in the days before hotels were known—was always sure of a welcome wherever he went.

That this image of themselves as hardy, independent pioneers is out-of-date, and has been out-of-date at least since World War I, makes it no less satisfying to the Afrikaners. Indeed, the very difference between the heroic life of the 19th Century trekker and the life of the average Afrikaner of today makes this image all the more compelling.

BY the end of World War I, there was virtually no unoccupied land left in South Africa that could be profitably farmed. Nor were the Boers skilled farmers, able to wring a living out of marginal land. Their custom had always been, when the land was exhausted by their crude farming and grazing methods, to move elsewhere. The result was that now—when there was nowhere left to move to—many became *bywoners* (livers beside) or sharecroppers, working for another man for a share of his farm's produce. They could not become out-and-out farm laborers since wage levels for such work were set by the black man, willing to toil long and hard for $10 or $15 a month, and frequently for much less. In any case, the Afrikaners *would* not become farm laborers since they considered such "Kaffir work" beneath their dignity. When agricultural prices fell in the years following the war, fewer and fewer Afrikaners could make a living from the land either as farm owners or sharecroppers, and they began to crowd into the towns.

In the towns, these uprooted farmers faced an equally harsh reality. Few of them had skills which would enable them to compete with the English-speaking townspeople, and here, as in the country, they would not compete for the unskilled labor done by the black man at near-starvation wages. To make matters worse, business in towns and cities was conducted mostly in English, a language they did not understand. It is impossible not to feel sympathy for these Afrikaners of the 1920s and 1930s who found themselves lost in the new century into which the world had moved. The whole of their education and upbringing, all the talk of their politicians and the sermons of their preachers, had been devoted to glorifying a way of life which had now become totally impossible.

OLDER South Africans remember and describe the look of this defeated Afrikaner ex-farmer, sitting dejectedly on the *stoep* of some battered villa in one of the poorer suburbs of Johannesburg, looking out over the passing traffic with the gaze of a man accustomed to the open veld and the mountain ranges. Not surprisingly, his resentment turned two ways. He resented the English-speaking who had arrived here first in the fields of mining, industry and commerce, and whose language seemed to have been raised as a barrier against him in his own land. And he resented the African, whose increasing skills he saw as a threat to his own future livelihood.

A huge "poor white" problem grew up—and nearly all the poor whites were Afrikaners. There were nearly 300,000 of them by the late 1920s. In the early 1930s, one man in five could be classed as belonging to this hopeless army of almost unemployable men. The problem of the poor whites has left an abiding mark on South African political thought, just as the Depression of the 1930s and the consequent unemployment still continue to affect American and British political thinking.

The coalition of the Nationalist and Labour Parties which came into power in 1924 tackled the problem with a new policy. Under their "civilized labor" plan, a host of jobs in government service were set aside exclusively for white men, and more important in its future consequences, the white man was insulated against the harsh working of economic laws by being paid at rates based on his needs "as a civilized person," instead of at the market value of his labor. In this way the pattern was set for all the "job reservation" laws and industrial legislation based on race which would be passed in future years to protect whites against black competition. During the 16 years between 1924 and 1940, great numbers of poor whites were absorbed into Government or provincial employment, many of them doing "Kaffir work," but working separately from black men and being paid wages which were sometimes 12 times as high as "Kaffir" pay.

Today, although the Afrikaners have expanded into many more fields of activity, this basic pattern of employment is still maintained. Afrikaners fill the overwhelming majority of Government posts: they are civil servants, clerks, policemen, schoolteachers and railway and post-office workers. Afrikaners also provide most of the manpower for South Africa's sizable and well-equipped Army and Air Force. In all, about one in five of all employable whites between the ages of 15 and 60 works for the central or the provincial governments, and almost all of them are Afrikaners. Their other principal field of employment remains farming.

The situation in farming is a complicated one, and is causing concern to Afrikaner intellectuals and politicians. It is still true that more than 80 per cent of all white farmers in South Africa are Afrikaners, but the number who actually live on and work the farms they own is dwindling fast. Dr. J. C. Neethling of the Government's Department of Agricultural Economics and Marketing was reported as saying in 1959 that nearly 5,500 farms in Natal and more than 2,000 in the Orange Free State which had been occupied in 1945 by whites had since been left entirely to the care of nonwhites. A Dutch Reformed Church survey, made some years ago, estimated that in some areas 30 to 40 per cent of all the farms were owned by absentee landlords.

The Nationalist Government has attempted to counteract this sustained flight from the land by "featherbedding" the farming industry. South Africa is not naturally an agricultural land. It is too dry and the soil is too thin. In general, the country's agriculture cannot compete successfully in world markets, and the domestic market is insufficient because three quarters of the population remains too poor to buy many farm products. The farmers, however, are the most powerful single voting bloc in Parliament, and in consequence, agriculture enjoys the benefit of guaranteed prices, preferential transport rates and huge export subsidies. Millions of subsidized bags of mealies (Indian corn), for example, which the Africans at home would be happy to eat if they had the money to pay for them, are sent to Red China. In 1961, South Africa shipped 24 million pounds of butter and eight million pounds of cheese to be sold overseas at a loss, the loss being made up by Government subsidies which, in turn, came from taxes levied on more profitable industries. All this keeps farmers prosperous but does little to further a much-needed modernization of the industry.

All these Government efforts, however, have not been successful in keeping the Afrikaner on the

THE AFRIKAANS LANGUAGE

The language of the Afrikaners and of most Cape Coloreds, Afrikaans developed from the 17th Century Dutch spoken by Cape Town's founders. It differs from its parent tongue primarily in two ways: a number of Afrikaans words are simply phonetic equivalents of expressions borrowed from African tribal languages and others, and Afrikaans grammar and spelling are simpler than the Dutch. Modern philologists generally agree that this simplification came about naturally: the language adapted itself to the needs of a people battling with a new and sometimes hostile environment. Long just an oral language, Afrikaans has been used in literature since 1875 and has been taught in schools since 1914. It became (with English) an official language of South Africa in 1925. Soon after, the Bible was translated into Afrikaans and a standard dictionary was compiled.

land. Instead, syndicates of city dwellers have bought up large blocks of land which they farm with black labor, while the original farming families abandon the country for the town. The census of 1951 showed that even then 70 per cent of all Afrikaners had become town or city dwellers, to whom the traditional way of life of their people was known, if known at all, only from an occasional weekend visit in a car.

BY the end of World War II, the problem of the poor whites had been overcome. Wartime prosperity aided the efforts which the Government had initiated, and most Afrikaners had secured jobs paying them enough to support a "civilized" standard of living. The average annual income of a white family rose by nearly 50 per cent between 1941 and 1955. That this gain had been achieved through political action was not lost on the Afrikaner. He made up his mind that from then on his people must be so organized that their full voting power could be brought to bear in their own interests.

During the 1920s and 1930s, a number of organizations were launched with the aim of molding all Afrikaners into a single, powerful group. The Federasie van Afrikaanse Kultuurverenigings, or Federation of Afrikaner Cultural Organizations, was set up in December 1929, with the backing of the Afrikaner secret society known as the Broederbond. In a short time the Federation's cultural activities had dwindled and it had become "the economic policy council of the *volk* as a whole." Characteristic of the aims of such organizations is a passage which appeared in a report issued by the Federation's Johannesburg branch. The report urges the good Afrikaner "to attend his Afrikaner church, speak Afrikaans everywhere, read Afrikaans books and papers, send his children to Afrikaans medium schools, go to Afrikaner *volk* celebrations, buy Afrikaner products, support Afrikaner businesses. . . ."

Another important Afrikaner organization, the Reddingsdaadbond, an economic-assistance society, was set up in 1938. Its aim was to mobilize the capital resources of the *volk* so that they could begin to compete with the English-speaking in such fields as banking and insurance. These efforts soon stimulated the expansion of such distinctly Afrikaner enterprises as Volkskas (a commercial bank), Sanlam (an insurance company) and the Federale Volksbelegging (an investment house).

The Afrikaners are proud of these expanding Afrikaner businesses, boasting of them and others like them in Government pamphlets. And certainly in the last decade there has been a remarkable breakthrough by Afrikaner businessmen into industry, finance and even—though to a much smaller extent—into mining. African millionaires—such as Jan Marais, Tom Muller and the tobacco magnate, Anton Rupert—have emerged, taking places alongside the several dozen millionaires of the English and Jewish communities. While the boom lasts, this process is certain to continue. But despite such signs of Afrikaner vigor, English-speaking South Africans still very largely control the country's industrial and commercial life.

The Afrikaners remain strongest in agriculture as well as in the industries based on agriculture, such as fruit and vegetable canning. They control 80 per cent of this prepared-foods' business, and the retail trade in the dorps, or small country towns, is almost entirely in their hands. In commerce as a whole, their total share may be well over 30 per cent.

THE modern Afrikaner, then, is increasingly a townsman, although he is still emotionally attached to the land and thinks of himself as heir to the rugged virtues of his trekker ancestors. He is less prosperous than his English-speaking counterpart but he feels much more a vital part of the life of his country. His support of his Government is wholehearted and almost filial, his political chiefs receiving the reverence given in other countries to great scientists, artists or military leaders. Though hospitable to strangers, he is parochial in outlook, requiring for complete acceptance that a man shall be Afrikaner by birth, Afrikaans in speech, a Nationalist in politics and a Calvinist in religion.

The Afrikaner is profoundly suspicious of what he regards as the "Coca-Cola and jukebox civilization" of the present day. He is deeply distrustful of generally accepted judgments, of things believed to be true everywhere else in the civilized world. The fact that a theory—such as evolution—is universally accepted is for the typical Afrikaner not proof of its rightness but evidence of its folly. Following a similar line of thinking—and one which is directly contrary to the general drift of world opinion—the Afrikaner believes that what is important about nations and races is not their similarities but their differences. It is the task of a people conscious of its destiny to preserve and even accentuate such differences. Compromise is therefore not the exercise of fairness and common sense but the betrayal of principle. Since the group, however, is the important unit, the same reasoning does not apply to individuals. While it is the group's duty to maintain absolute independence, it is the individual's duty to submerge his independence in the group.

It is in line with such thinking that all Afrikaner organizations—political, religious, educational, financial, cultural and sporting—have much the same aims. In many cases the same people are leaders in a number of totally different fields. All work together, as if under a single central direction, to secure the advancement of the *volk*. "It seems," said a visiting writer to a well-known Afrikaner journalist, "that you wish your own people to be dominant in everything from Rugby football to nuclear science, and from folk-dancing to life insurance. Can that really be the case?" "Of course," the journalist answered instantly. "What else does 'nationalism' mean?"

ABSOLUTELY convinced of the rightness, even the righteousness, of his cause, the Afrikaner seldom, if ever, doubts the wisdom of his Government's policies toward the African. When others criticize, they are dismissed as fools who do not understand the situation. "If the world doesn't approve of what we are doing, if the United Nations wants to tell us how to run our country, then they can be damned. They don't know a thing about Africa and Africans. We do." Revealing in this connection are the words of Prime Minister Hendrik F. Verwoerd to South Africa's Parliament in January 1964. He believed, he said, that the world would one day realize South Africa is right in rejecting multiracialism, which is leading to the downfall of white civilization. "I maintain that the international position today is proof that this world of ours is sick. South Africa's duty is not to be drawn into this sickbed. Even if we are accused of isolating ourselves, it is our first duty to . . . ensure our survival, because that way we can perhaps provide the world with a remedy for its own sickness."

The Afrikaner's aim, then, is to secure his own position in South Africa by the drastic use of legislation and—should the moment come—by force of arms. His fear is of the *swart gevaar,* or black menace—the fear that the black man will arise in his millions and sweep away not only the Afrikaner people but their language, culture, institutions, their whole way of life.

This aim and this fear are combined in the words of a farmer in the northern Transvaal who stroked his favorite rifle as he spoke. "If all else fails, at least I have got this to rely on. And if the Kaffirs don't behave themselves, they will get what's coming to them. They will never succeed in making one of their Congos in South Africa."

SELF-RIGHTEOUSNESS, virtually all philosophers and moralists agree, tends to harden men's hearts and make them blind. And what is, or appears to be, necessity has been used by many peoples to justify acts which in the eyes of history appear wanton and cruel. The nations of the world, speaking collectively through the United Nations, have strongly condemned South Africa's treatment of its black population. But the Afrikaners, convinced of their God-given superiority to the black man, justified by their mission of *creating* their nation and goaded by fear of the *swart gevaar,* cannot perceive that their treatment of the country's more than 15 million nonwhites is cruel to the point of inhumanity.

They do not see that laws passed by their legislature have progressively robbed the African of what few rights he possessed—rights essential to his dignity as a man. The acute political analyst Hannah Arendt, in her book on the trial of Adolf Eichmann, suggests that the essence of the Nazis' crime against the Jews was a refusal to "share the earth" with another group of human beings. The actions of South Africa's Afrikaner-controlled Government cannot, of course, be compared with the insane program of genocide practiced by the Nazis, but they do smack of a similarly cold and inhuman refusal to "share the earth" with a vast number of their fellow human creatures.

An old Afrikaner farmer and his wife stand beside the rough walls of their house on the Little Karroo in southern Cape Province.

Bulwarks of Conservatism in the Modern World

The Afrikaners, largely of Dutch descent, form the majority of South Africa's white population. They make up 80 per cent of the nation's white farmers, and gerrymandering of voting districts gives them the most powerful voice in Parliament. In return for their support, every government seeks to please these rural voters and to bolster the country's sagging agriculture through subsidies. Tough and hard-working, the Afrikaner farmer is individualistic among his equals and paternalistic toward those he regards as his inferiors—the Coloreds and Africans. Many English-speaking whites hold the same racial attitudes as the Afrikaners, but with less virulence. Although the wealthy and urban Afrikaners mix with other whites, they still see themselves as part of a distinct people with a cherished language and tradition.

PRECIOUS WATER SUPPLY is inspected by Gerrit Visser on his 6,000-acre sheep farm on the Great Karroo. The farmer's three wells provide ample insurance against recurring drought.

IMPROMPTU GAME delights Mr. Visser's son and nephew and two African boys, children of hired hands. In rural areas, white and African children generally play together until school age.

AFTERNOON REFRESHMENT of fruit and cool drinks *(below)* is enjoyed by the Visser family on the lawn near the farmhouse. The farm is named De Aar Plaas—"the farm on the water vein."

SHEEP FARMER leads a quiet but arduous and isolated existence with his large family

WOOL SHEARING, which occurs every 10 months, is done by Colored workers who go from farm to farm and receive seven cents per sheep. Each sheep yields nine or 10 pounds of wool.

WELL-KEPT HERD of South African merino sheep is corralled by Mr. Visser *(below)*. The sheep have a heavy, fine-fibered fleece except during drought, when the quality is apt to suffer.

TWO GENERATIONS of a large English-speaking family, the Arthur Amms *(above),* drink tea with friends in their farmhouse in the northern Transvaal. The Amms raise citrus fruits in the warm region.

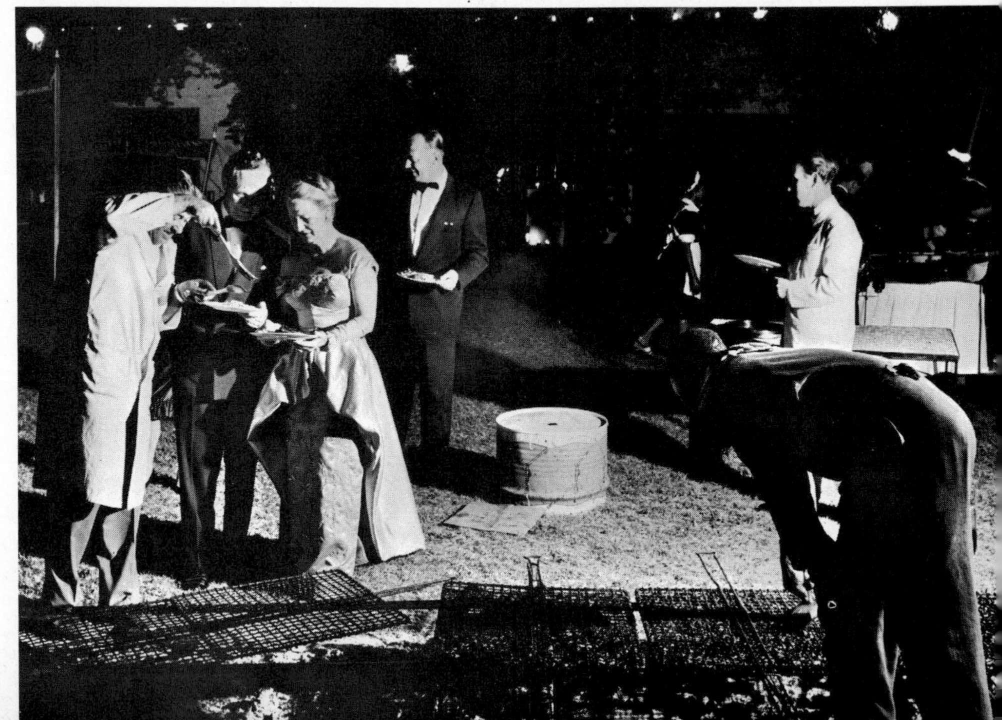

OUTDOOR BARBECUE, a South African custom, attracts Cape Town society to the estate of Abe Bloomberg, once Cape Town's mayor. The woman at left is the director of the University of Cape Town Ballet.

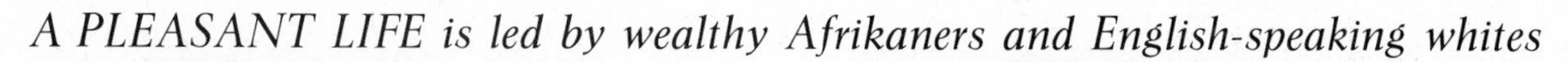

A PLEASANT LIFE is led by wealthy Afrikaners and English-speaking whites

DRINKS AFTER TENNIS in a Johannesburg suburb are sipped by the English-speaking hostess, Mrs. Thelma Bothner *(right),* and the wives of two industrialists, one Austrian *(left),* the other Hungarian.

CANDLELIGHT DINNER on New Year's Eve brings a crowd to a banquet hall in South Africa's most elegant hotel, the Mount Nelson in Cape Town. The holiday season comes at the year's hottest time.

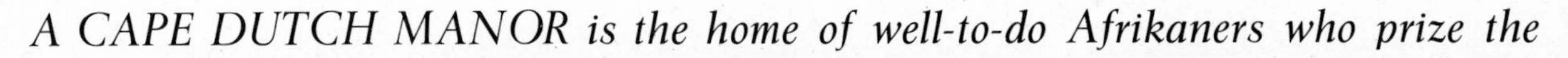

A CAPE DUTCH MANOR is the home of well-to-do Afrikaners who prize the

PROSPEROUS FAMILY, the N. C. Krones, who own extensive vineyards in the southwestern part of Cape Province, gather in front of the fireplace in their beamed living room. The three generations of the family include *(left to right):* Mrs. Gertruda Krone, her son, grandson, husband and daughter-in-law. The house was originally built by Mrs. Krone's ancestors in 1719.

massive simplicity of their surroundings

CHRISTMAS SERENADE marks the holiday season on the farm, with Colored workers singing to members of the Krone family, who listen attentively on the veranda of their home.

TEENAGE PARTY marking the return of 16-year-old Louise Krone from school draws her friends from the countryside. Unlike the Krones, many Afrikaners disapprove of such dancing.

PROUD WINEGROWERS, N. C. Krone Jr. and his son *(right)* sample prizewinning vintages in their wine cellar. South Africa's first vintners were 17th Century French Huguenot immigrants.

HARMONIOUS LINES define the architecture of the Krones' house. Its name, Twee Jonge Gezellen, means "Two Young Friends," recalling the friendship of the men who built it in 1719. Many old Cape Dutch houses are preserved as monuments. Groote Schuur (Big Barn), built by Cecil Rhodes, is the official Cape Town residence of South Africa's prime ministers.

COOL HALLWAY with white plaster walls and polished tile floors *(below)* leads to an open door at the Krone farm. Cape Dutch houses were constructed of whatever materials were available—unbaked bricks and plaster, reed thatch, and even teak from the hulls of vessels shipwrecked along the coast. The clean, uncluttered design creates an atmosphere of chaste elegance.

SWIMMING POOL at Twee Jonge Gezellen is a cool retreat for the Krone children on a hot afternoon. Although the pool is a modern addition to the grounds, it is a replica of a garden pool at Groot Constantia, the most famous Cape Dutch manor house. In the distance lie the Krone vineyards. Wine from the Krone farm, like most South African wine, is sold mainly in Britain.

AFRICAN NURSEMAID carries her small charge on a beach at Durban, providing amusement with a ball. The beach is segregated, but nonwhite nannies are allowed. As in the U.S. South, many white children in South Africa are tended by black women.

6

Apartheid in Action

A COMPLETELY new chapter of South African history opened with the general election of 1948. During and immediately after World War II, the Africans' hopes for political progress had been fired by wartime slogans about freedom and democracy, and by the United Nations' proclamations in favor of human rights and fundamental freedom without distinction of race. Moreover, in the British colonies to the north, Africans had begun to participate in governing their own homelands. Black South Africans decided they would "urgently demand the granting of full citizenship rights such as are enjoyed by all Europeans in South Africa." When, therefore, during the election campaign of 1948, the Nationalists, then out of power, put forward the policy of "apartheid," or complete separation of the races, their program had a powerful appeal for white South Africans frightened by these threats to their supremacy over 10 million nonwhite fellow citizens.

Though the Nationalists did not secure a majority of votes, they did secure a small majority of seats in Parliament and at once began to translate their program into action.

Apartheid was not a new policy. It was a modification of a policy as old as the Dutch settlement in South Africa, the policy known as *baasskap*. *Baasskap* (which can be translated as "bosshood") meant simply white domination. The modification now proposed was an increased degree of separation between the races. This separation would be carried right through the country's political, economic and social life. Black men would not vote on the same roll or for the same Parliament as whites. They would not do the same jobs, or not do them together—and certainly not for the same pay. Above all, they would live in different areas from the whites, and every law that could be devised to keep the races totally apart would be enacted and enforced.

There was one big snag, however. The white man could not do without the black man's labor. It was needed on the farms, in the workshops and factories, on the docks, on the railroads, on road construction gangs—and in kitchens and nurseries. It was needed above all in the mines. So the separation was never a complete partition: it was an exclusion. Dr. Daniel F. Malan, who was Prime Minister from 1948 to 1954 and under whom apartheid was established, was quite explicit: "Theoretically," he wrote, "the object of the policy of Apartheid could be achieved by dividing the country into two parts with all the Whites in one and all the Blacks in the other. For the foreseeable future however this is simply not practical politics."

THE effect of apartheid on the black man, therefore, is that in the name of racial separation, he has been stripped of whatever political rights he previously possessed. Laws have been passed which restrict the work he may do and the places where he may live. They decide whether or not his wife and children may live with him. In 70 per cent of the country, the laws reduce him to the status of a temporary migrant who can be forced to leave his home on the mere say-so of an official. Mr. Michiel C. Botha, Minister of Bantu Administration and Development, made no bones about it when he said: "It is . . . the duty of every official entrusted with the task of Bantu Administration sedulously to apply the basic principle . . . that the Bantu's stay in the white areas can be justified only by the need for his services there."

When the Malan Government came to power in 1948, one of its main concerns was to remove some 48,000 Colored voters from the common Parliamentary roll. It planned to do this through the Separate Representation of Voters Bill, which would allow the Colored to be enrolled on a separate list and to elect four whites to represent their interests in Parliament. This proposal cut directly across an entrenched clause in the Constitution. The bill caused a prolonged constitutional crisis, and did not finally become law until 1956. A further step—abolition of the last vestiges of African representation in Parliament (there had been seven white "natives' representatives")—was taken under Dr. Verwoerd in 1959.

IN the meantime, the Nationalists produced a spate of legislation designed not only to achieve increased separation of the races but also to render the African legally and economically powerless. Among the first were laws ensuring that segregation would be enforced in places where it had long been merely customary, and in some where it had not been customary at all. Black and white were to be kept apart in parks, railroad stations, buses, post offices, beaches and clubs, and in all other public buildings. They had long been kept apart by custom in hotels, restaurants, theaters and cinemas. Now they would be kept apart by law.

Though enforcement of these new segregation laws is strict, common sense and business interest produce curious anomalies. Nearly all small cafés, for instance, serve Africans but do not allow them to sit at tables. Though nonwhites must go to separate counters for postage stamps or railroad tickets, they may circulate and buy freely in the big department stores—but are not allowed to have a cup of tea in the stores' restaurants or make use of the lavatories.

The biggest anomaly of all is that, though few white South Africans would admit a black into their homes on social terms, nearly all white children are brought up by black nursemaids, and a white lady does not object to being brought her breakfast in bed by a black manservant, or to having him do her personal washing. The explanation of this is that, though the principles of apartheid may appear to be flouted, those of *baasskap* are being maintained, since the relation is that of servant and master.

With the same aim of separation in view, the Prohibition of Mixed Marriages Act was passed in 1949—"to check blood mixture and promote racial purity"—and a year later an "Immorality Act" was passed imposing severe penalties for sexual intercourse between whites and all nonwhites.

Since it was now a crime for people of different racial groups to marry or to have sexual relations, it was necessary for the authorities to know with certainty to which racial group every person in the country belonged. In 1950, therefore, the Population Registration Act was passed, ordering the classification of the whole population and the issue of identity cards. On the borderline between "White" and "Colored" a number of personal tragedies occurred. White husbands found that the wives they had lived with as "Whites" were now officially classified as "Colored," and vice versa. Families were split in half when children of the same parents were placed under different headings. A special board was formed to decide—by such arbitrary tests as curliness of hair, skin color, thickness of lips, and the general opinion of the neighbors—to which race doubtful cases were to be assigned. By 1963, 13 years after passage of the law, 21,000 borderline cases were still waiting for a decision on their status.

ALL attempts to modify these laws that aim at "racial purity," because of the many human tragedies they have occasioned, have met with intense opposition. When an Afrikaans magazine interviewed prominent Afrikaners on the question several years ago, Professor H. J. Venter of the University of Pretoria took the opportunity to declare that there was no alternative to the Immorality Act and that offenders should be imprisoned for long periods. If this failed, the professor said, they could be emasculated, because in any case they were "poor human material." The women interviewed, two highly respectable Afrikaner matrons, also believed that the offending males should be made to undergo an operation. The Rev. E.J.L. Norval, a minister of one of the Dutch Reformed Churches, thought the same result should be achieved by other means. Emasculation, he said, is not permissible, because the Lord said man must multiply. Instead, offenders should be imprisoned for life, or perhaps hanged.

Another sphere into which the Government introduced its ideas of apartheid was that of education. In general, the races had always been segregated in school. But though black education could be called a poor copy of the white, it had at least been on similar lines and worked toward similar standards. Now, however, in the Bantu Education Act of 1953, the Government took over control from the provincial authorities and introduced plans for a specifically "African" type of education, designed to train Africans for the positions in life they would be required to fill under apartheid. Though the provinces had controlled education and administered the state's financial aid, about 90 per cent of African schools belonged to missions. These bodies were now faced with the alternative of accepting the Government's Bantu education program or foregoing subsidies. For a while, the churches opposed the measure bitterly, but in the end they either gave in to the Government or closed their schools. Only a few, the Roman Catholics in particular, raised money to try to maintain their independence.

The effect of Government control has been that more African children receive some education, but it is inferior in quality. School attendance has risen markedly but, critics point out, this increase has been achieved mainly by holding double sessions in the first two grades, with the same teacher instructing two sets of pupils. Classes are grossly overcrowded and books are scarce. Moreover, since the Government's financial contribution to Bantu education is fixed by law, the more children receiving some share of education, the lower the quality of that education must necessarily be. The amount spent annually per African pupil actually fell from $25 to $18.72 in one decade. In January 1961 the late Dr. A. B. Xuma, a renowned African leader, pointed out that the state was spending "eight times as much per head per white pupil as it did per African pupil."

THE same policy is being carried out at the university level. Of the nine universities in South Africa, two—Cape Town and Witwatersrand (in Johannesburg)—until recently admitted non-Europeans to the same teaching facilities and student societies as whites, though social contacts were restricted. Two of the other universities were open to nonwhites, though with mainly segregated facilities. The so-called "Extension of University Education Act" of 1959 provided for gradual elimination of nonwhites from all white universities. In 1961 "Wits" still had 258 nonwhite students, but five years later only three Africans were left at Cape Town University and six at "Wits." The new policy has involved the setting up of five university colleges, three for the main African tribal groups, and one each for the Coloreds and Indians. These institutions are completely controlled by the Government, which appoints all instructors and administrative officers, and they lack many of the resources available at established universities.

STILL another area in which the African has suffered from increasingly restrictive legislation since 1948 is the economic. Legal discrimination against the African as a worker is no new thing in South Africa. As far back as 1926 a "Colour Bar Act" was passed which prevented Africans from obtaining skilled mining jobs. Thirty years later, in 1956, the Minister of Labor secured power under the so-called Industrial Conciliation Act to reserve *any* class of work for any particular racial group. The decrees since issued, coupled with longstanding prejudice and trade union regulations, have developed into a complex network of restrictions which forbid Africans to do almost any work which can be classed as "skilled." Some of these restrictions border on the whimsical. For example, an African may prepare a wall for painting but he cannot apply the paint—unless he is painting a building in a rural area or in one of his own segregated townships. In the Transvaal he is allowed to drive a meat truck of up to a certain weight but not beyond it (heavy trucking for some reason is a job reserved for whites). In certain cities he may act as an elevator man in a "black" building but not in a "white" one.

The same result is achieved from the opposite end, simply by making it almost impossible for Africans to be enrolled as apprentices and so preventing them from acquiring skills. In consequence, only a small percentage of the skilled workers in South Africa are nonwhite—that is, African, Colored or Asian—though these groups together outnumber the whites by more than four to one, and the Coloreds, in particular, are generally admitted to make excellent artisans.

That the black man in "white" areas is almost entirely confined to unskilled or semiskilled work is only a small part of his disabilities. Even in the work he is allowed to do he cannot effectively combine to improve pay or conditions. Since 1953 Africans have not been admitted into registered trade unions—a further way of preventing them from acquiring skills. The Industrial Conciliation Act of 1956 also forbade the establishment of any more "mixed" unions of white and nonwhite workers, and in those which exist, nonwhites are compelled to hold separate meetings and only whites can be elected to executive positions. Moreover, under the Native Labour Regulation Act of 1911, it is a criminal offense for an African to disobey an order from his boss or foreman, or even to quit his job. This act, coupled with the still more stringent legislation enacted during the past few years, renders the African economically defenseless. It is not surprising, therefore, to find that his wage levels are low and his tenure in his job precarious.

THE Africans, for the better part of a century, have provided the heavy labor in the gold and diamond mines, which have largely created the country's wealth. Yet in 1963 the average cash wage for an African miner worked out to approximately $213 a year, with food, housing, medical attention and some clothing supplied free. In domestic service in urban areas African servants earn from $16 to $32 a month, with food and accommodations as a rule provided. In country areas, the so-called platteland, wages are still lower. John Nkosi, an African journalist, writing in the Johannesburg *Star,* gave the example of an elderly servant in a rural area who was earning $5.60 a month and who pleaded for an increase in her wages. "After the maid had pointed out her home responsibilities and the inadequacies of her earnings, her employer agreed to add $1.40 a month to her salary—provided that in future she bought her own uniform."

Even in urban areas the situation is not much better. An African laborer's monthly wage in the building industry of Pretoria averaged $44.30 in the 1960s. This means that he received between one fifth and one sixth of the wages paid to carpenters, bricklayers, plumbers and painters, all jobs reserved exclusively for whites in the "white" areas of the city. Although the economic expansion of recent years has drawn an increasing number of nonwhites into industrial employment, the black man's position relative to the white worker is still strikingly depressed.

South African Government propagandists frequently claim that the standard of living of Africans in South Africa is the highest on the continent. Critics reply that in view of the fact that South Africa is by far the wealthiest area on the continent, it would be strange if African workers received no benefit from the country's wealth, or from their long association with Western civilization. But they also refer to such reports as No. 172 of the Council for Social and Industrial Research—and more recent investigations by the South African Institute of Race Relations—which show that a very high proportion of African families in the main urban centers live below the "poverty datum line" —that is, in a situation of acute need. And the workers in the main urban centers are, by general admission, the best paid in the country.

Medical figures support the Council's findings. The incidence of malnutrition diseases in parts of South Africa is grimly high. African children between the ages of one and four die at an estimated 13 times the rate of white children in the same age group. The medical health officer in Port Elizabeth reported in 1962 that, on an average, 50 nonwhite children died monthly in the Livingstone Hospital alone because of malnutrition. During 1963, of new tuberculosis cases reported, 1,213 were whites and 57,401 Africans. Tuberculosis decreased by 7 per cent among white children and increased by 20.3 per cent among African children. Relating the incidence of the disease to poverty and bad housing, the medical health officer of Pretoria said: "At present, economic circumstances force many sufferers to work until they literally drop dead."

A POET'S VIEW OF THE MINES

An uncompromising picture of the plight of the African mineworker is given in an impressive poem by the great Zulu poet B. W. Vilakazi, who died in 1947. Two stanzas of this poem, "In the Gold Mines," translated from the Zulu "Ezinkomponi," appear below.

Roar, without rest, machines of the mines,
Roar from dawn till darkness falls;
I shall wake, oh, let me be!
Roar, machines, continue deaf
To black men groaning as they labor—
Tortured by their aching muscles,
Gasping in the fetid air,
Reeking from the dirt and sweat—
Shaking themselves without effect.

My brother is with me, carrying
His pick and shovel on his shoulder,
And, on his feet, are heavy boots.
He follows me toward the shaft:
The earth will swallow us who burrow,
And, if I die there, underground,
What does it matter? Who am I?
Dear Lord! All round me, every day,
I see men stumble, fall and die.

What is the situation in the countryside? Travelers passing through the Reserves, particularly the Transkei, first of the Government's newly created Bantustans, are struck by the beauty of the landscape and the fine bearing of the people, and Government-sponsored publications speak with enthusiasm of these "happy picturesque people living the most carefree existence imaginable," and of their "carefree idyllic existence in their little thatched huts." Those who look closer see a different picture. When the *Rand Daily Mail* in 1962 conducted investigations into several drought-stricken Reserves, they found that the incidence of pellagra and other deficiency diseases was increasing, and that hundreds of people were on the verge of starvation. Their reports were denounced by the Minister of Bantu Administration as "unfavourable and distorted." Where any malnutrition does exist, he explained, it is "due to wrong eating habits." The Government did, however, distribute emergency rations in drought-stricken areas.

The principal stated aim of apartheid is, of course, "to move the blacks increasingly out of the 'white' areas, and confine them more and more to the 12-13 per cent of the land area allotted to them." In this aim, the successive Nationalist Governments since 1948 have had little success. In 1951 there were 2,328,534 Africans living in urban areas. Only nine years later the figure had risen to 3,471,233, and in 1965 it was admitted to be approaching five million. Plainly the economic forces which draw the African toward the white-occupied areas, and particularly toward the cities, are proving much stronger than the legislation designed to keep them where they are or to drive them back.

This legislation consists mainly of the so-called "pass laws," the Group Areas Act, the Natives

(Urban Areas) Act, and provisions making it impossible for the African to own land in urban areas. The "pass laws" are designed to restrict the freedom of movement of Africans. Their basic principle is that all African adults (including women) must possess a "pass," a passportlike document giving pertinent facts about its bearer. This must be carried with him at all times, and produced on demand for any policeman or authorized official. The primary aim of the pass laws is to control the influx of Africans into urban areas; secondary purposes are to prevent an African from deserting his job and to make it easier to track down criminals. Criminals, however, have no more difficulty in securing the necessary documents in South Africa than elsewhere.

WHAT the pass laws, buttressed by additional legislation passed in the spring of 1964, have done is to make it more and more difficult for Africans to establish permanent homes in urban areas. Large numbers of women, with their children, have been sent away from the towns, and many more thousands have been refused permission to accompany their husbands there. These laws are bitterly hated by the Africans, and from the economic point of view their effect is negative: they provide a serious obstacle to the free flow of labor, and increasingly will prevent the formation of a settled and responsible labor force. In addition, by depriving the worker of any *right* to remain in an urban area, by making his stay conditional on his labor being required by the white man, and by putting all kinds of obstacles in the way of his establishing a home of his own and of gathering his family around him, they add enormous burdens to the conditions of unrest and endless anxiety in the daily life of the urban African.

The Group Areas Act of 1950, as its name implies, was designed to establish segregated areas in which all Africans (and other nonwhites) were obliged to live. Implementation of the act has inevitably involved the uprooting of thousands of nonwhite families who were living in areas now designated as "white." However, this massive relocation has had a beneficial byproduct. Since 1948 the Nationalist Governments have built or subsidized vast new housing developments for Africans. Slums and shantytowns have been swept away on an impressive scale. Between 1948 and 1968 the Nationalist government's policies have resulted in more than 250,000 houses being built at a total cost estimated at $420 million.

A great deal of the good these measures would have achieved, however, has been thwarted by the Government's determination that all Africans outside the Reserves are to be regarded only as "temporary migrants," whose presence depends solely on their usefulness. In accordance with this principle, the African is debarred from owning land in most of the new developments and can be turned out of his home if he loses his job, or simply by an official's administrative decision.

This ever-growing structure of laws makes the Africans and the other nonwhites virtual exiles in their own land. They live an entirely different life from that of white South Africans and, such is the separation of the peoples, a life which not one in a hundred whites knows anything about. It is, to be plain, the life of the underdog. Hemmed round by regulations framed for them alone, the Africans are chivvied by officials and continually harassed by the police. "Waar's jou 'pass,' jong?" ("Where's your pass, boy?"), the police will say, and if it's hanging in a coat at home, the African will be lucky if he gets off with only a fine.

THE life of the black man is one of perpetual insecurity. He is insecure in his job: an angry word or a quick answer can put him out immediately. So can suspicion. If money or goods are missing, few employers will worry about proof. He is insecure of tenure in his home. If an official finds an African "idle or undesirable," or suspects him of political interests ("that man's a troublemaker"), the official can send him back to his "rural area"—which the African may not have seen for 30 years and where he may have neither friends nor relatives.

Ill health, too, is a lurking enemy; an African can be sent back to his so-called "homeland" ("endorsed out" is the dreaded phrase) for being medically unfit. Since his only justification for being in an urban area is the work he is doing, if he can't work, he has no justification. And then there is his wife. The fact that a working man—with endless difficulty

—has gotten permission from a labor bureau to take a job in, say, Johannesburg, does not entitle his wife to come along and keep house for him in one of the city's suburbs.

Nor is it only the white man who makes life a burden for the Africans. Black men prey on blacks. Ambitious Africans, unable to rise above menial jobs—and so unable to buy the things they long for, such as big cars, women, admiration, drink, fine clothes—turn criminal. In 1962, 2,055 Africans were convicted of murder, attempted murder or culpable homicide. Another 24,725 were convicted of aggravated assault, 39,113 of common assault and 61,551 of robbery or theft. Of every 1,000 Africans in the population, six were convicted during 1962 of serious crime and 73 of nonserious crime (including pass-law offenses).

As is natural when, on the average, one African in every 13 is convicted each year for a trivial offense—failure to carry a pass or some breach of location rules—the law falls into contempt. Imprisonment brings no disgrace. Many Africans inside prisons, especially the political leaders, are heroes. So too are the payroll robbers and hijackers of truckloads of cigarettes—big-time gangsters who prey on whites. Only the *tsotsis* are hated. These are small-time thugs who jostle home-going Africans into doorways on payday, or hold a man up in a crowded train with sharpened knitting needles. Yet no one dreams of going to the police. "First, it'll do you no good," the Africans say, "and second, the cops are more our enemies than the *tsotsis*." What *can* an African do then? "Hide your cash on payday where it's hard to find. Leave a quid where *tsotsis* can get it easily. Trust to luck that they won't knife you."

TWO things in the African's life are endlessly strange. One is the utter remoteness of that life from the white world. The races see each other daily, hourly, every minute—only they never meet. It is as though the whites were living under glass. Cut off in this way, they seem to have no knowledge of and no interest in the *quality* of life lived by the Africans. "I know the blacks!" declares the foreman, or the police sergeant, or the mine boss—who has probably never spoken to an African below a shout. Even the administrators and clergymen whose direct concern is said to be to help the Africans are content to mutter their official reassurance: "Separate development. . . . Reach fulfilment on their own lines. . . . Bold experiment. . . . Wages higher than in Mozambique or Ghana. . . . Africans come to work in mines from as far away as Tanganyika, so obviously they must be happy. . . ."

It is not too farfetched to imagine the Africans enjoying "a carefree idyllic existence in their little thatched huts" in the Transkei, although, in fact, the Africans in the Reserves are largely undernourished and ill clothed. But it is hard to understand how whites can imagine the miners to be happy in their crowded mine compounds, without women or the sight of their families for six months or a year. Or the urban Africans in their segregated locations outside the cities, living among 10,000 decent little boxlike houses, all identical. Or in their horrible shantytowns, such as Windermere or Pimville.

THE second strangeness about African life is that despite—or perhaps because of—the ferocity and callousness with which he is surrounded, the African lives with a verve and a vigor matched by few other people in the world. What does the black man say of whites? "They don't know how to enjoy themselves by day or night." But the African knows how to enjoy himself with fervor. He flings himself into his rare enjoyments as Londoners flung themselves into their enjoyments during the blitz in World War II, and perhaps for the same reason.

In the suburbs of Johannesburg, a pennywhistle band has only to start playing on a Saturday afternoon for the pavement to be filled with jiving couples, delivery boys, housemaids, nursemaids. A township party, lasting all night, is an experience to remember. At a deeper level, the Africans of South Africa are beginning to create a popular music, a literature and an art unmatched on the continent until one reaches Nigeria.

Africans themselves detest any reference to their capacity for enjoyment. "Oh, so *you've* fallen for that 'happy black man' stuff," they will say. But it is true that, as in New York's Harlem, life in the locations is sometimes enlivened by a gaiety and joy that the prudent, calculating white man seems to have lost in South Africa and all over the world.

LONG QUEUE of African workers waits patiently at a Johannesburg bus stop. Commuting from distant segregated townships on buses and trains sometimes takes four hours each way.

UNPAVED STREET in Pimville, a slum "location" outside Johannesburg *(below)*, surges with life. Women carry water pails from public pumps since Pimville's houses lack plumbing.

The Bitter, Difficult Life of the Black Majority

The life of the black man in South Africa, especially in the cities, is beset by appalling difficulties. Segregation in its most extreme form—under the name of apartheid—rules every aspect of his existence. Many kinds of jobs are forbidden to him, and when he does find employment, he receives only a fraction of the pay a white man would get for the same work. He is forced to live in a segregated township, usually on the distant outskirts of the city where he works. His home is likely to be depressing, part of a drab housing project. He is so hemmed in by laws that he cannot quit his job, or choose a new one, or form a union, or go on strike. The police are ever ready to lock him up for any one of a hundred trivial offenses. Yet somehow, despite such heartbreaking obstacles, Africans can be cheerful and vivacious, their natural ebullience and warmth overcoming the rancor and the despair that would otherwise dominate them.

A barefoot African schoolboy jokes with neighbors in a Pimville alley. Throughout the country, schools for Africans are inadequate.

HOUSING DEVELOPMENTS, though often crowded and monotonous, are a vast

improvement over the old slums

NURSERY-SCHOOL CHILDREN in bright smocks dance and sing a Zulu song with their teacher, Beauty Mazibuko. This day nursery, or crèche, is in a section of the development near Johannesburg called Soweto. Crèches, designed primarily to care for the children of working mothers, have many pupils, but only three per cent of African children ever reach high school.

PATCHWORK OF ROOFS in Soweto, a complex of African townships, stretches away below a group of hospital workers who are taking an afternoon "beer break." Covering more than 25 square miles of the dusty veld, Soweto's pillbox houses shelter more than 700,000 Africans. The average Soweto house has running water but no indoor bathroom or electricity.

LEISURE TIME is spent in a variety of games or, by mineworkers living far from home, in desultory talk

GOLD-MINE WORKERS sit outside a grimly utilitarian barracks within a mine compound where they live while employed. Most miners work for about a year and then return home to their native villages.

YOUNG SOCCER PLAYERS chase a flying ball *(opposite)* near a number of Zulu huts in western Natal. Africans have enthusiastically adopted Western sports, even though they are excluded from white teams.

SIDEWALK LOUNGERS in Stellenbosch, a town in Cape Province, watch three Colored men play a game of "snooker." The Coloreds—people with mixed ancestry—enjoy a few rights denied to the Africans.

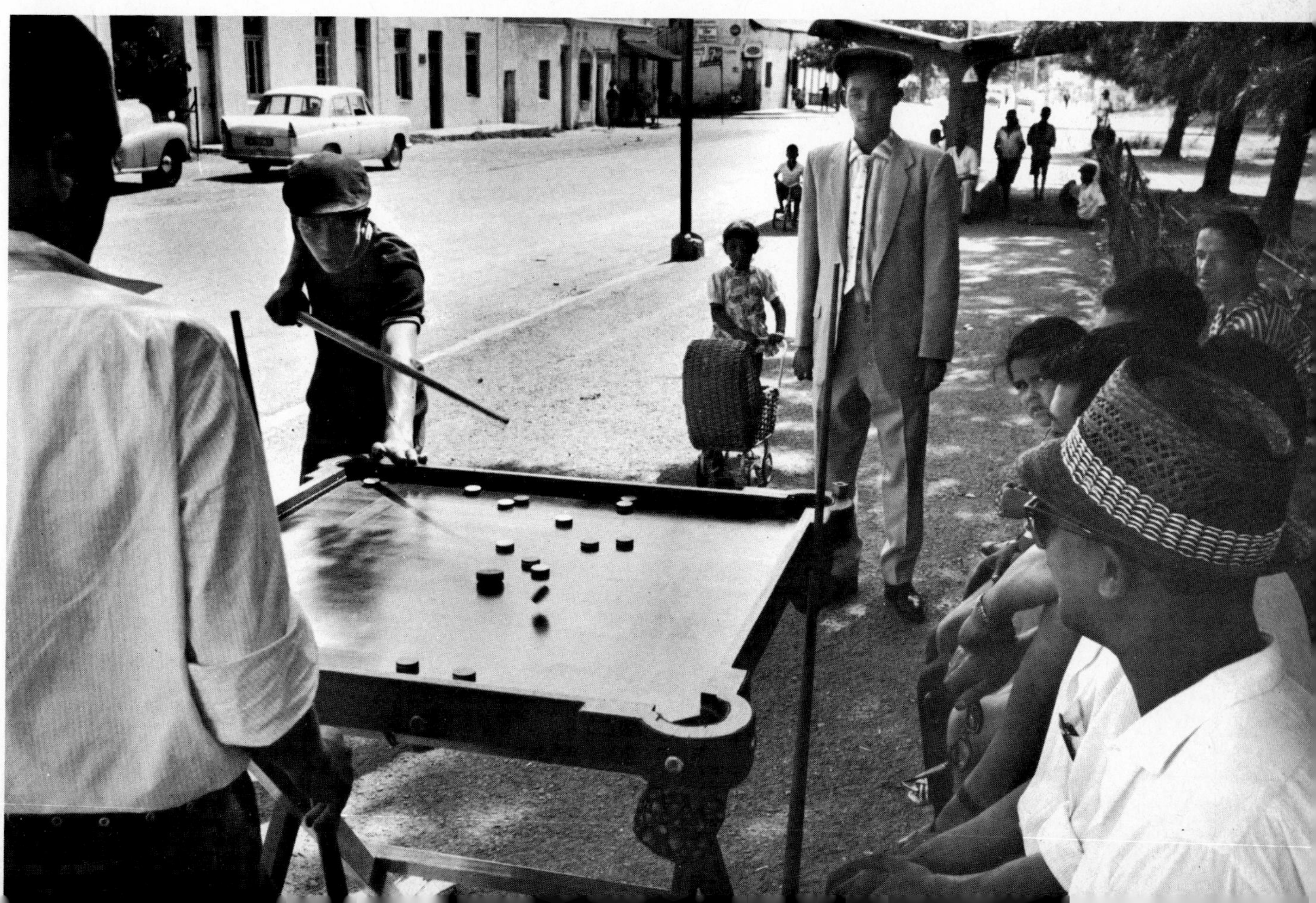

MEDICAL TRAINING, like other types of higher education, is open to a tiny

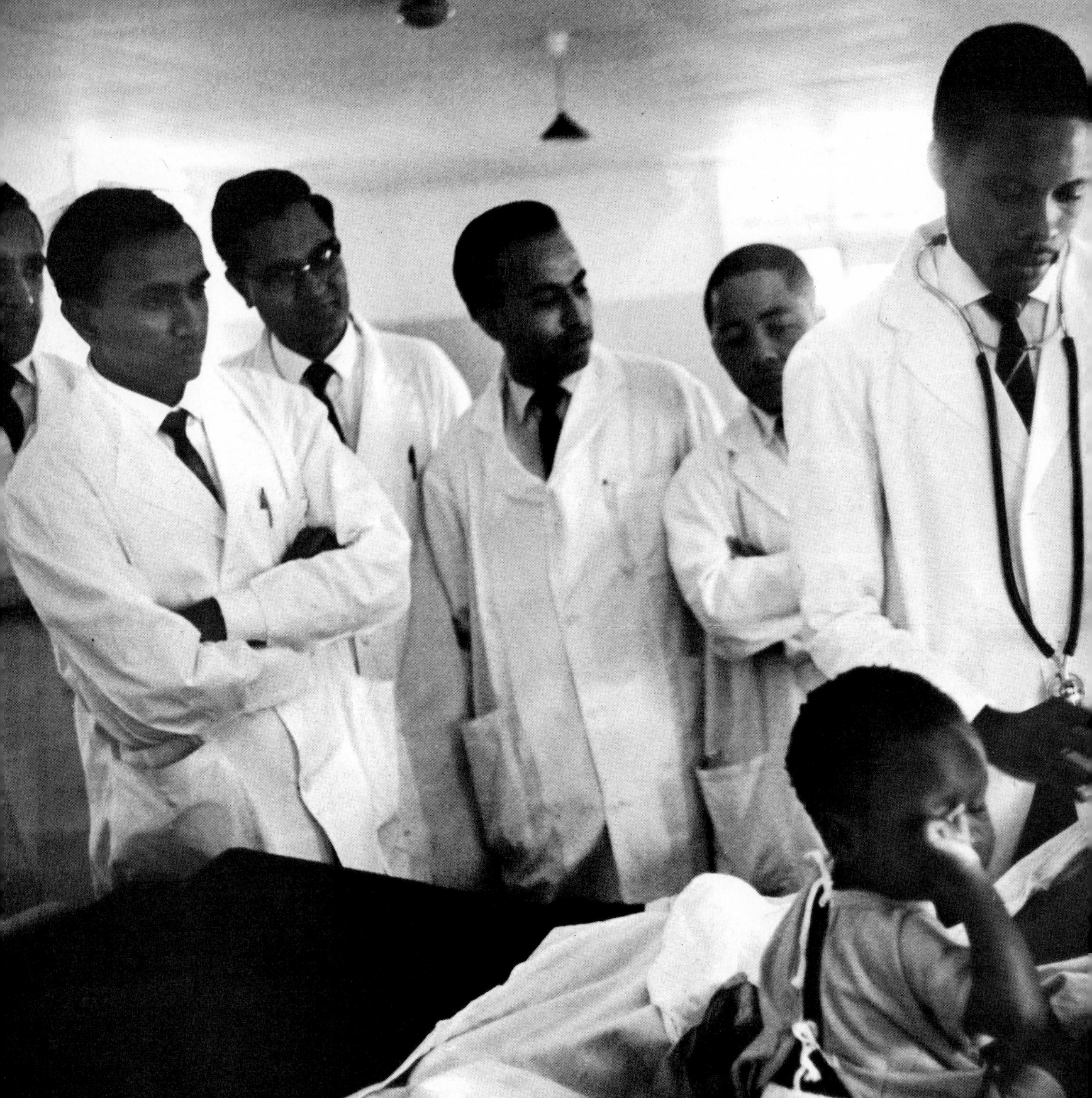

proportion of the nonwhite population

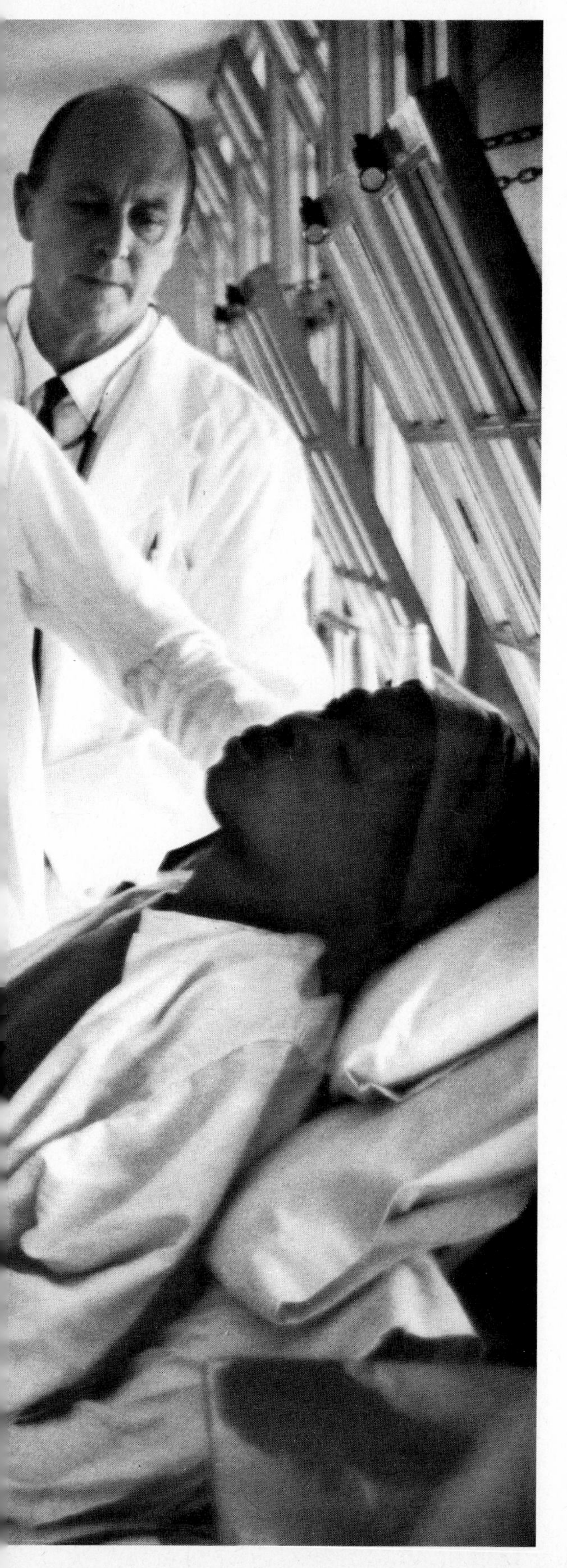

INDIAN STUDENT watches as a professor checks his work in a chemistry lab at the University College for Indians near Durban, the only college for South Africa's half million Asians.

AFRICAN INTERN examines a patient in a Durban hospital *(left)* as other non-European interns and a white doctor look on. In 1966 there were only 120 nonwhite doctors in South Africa.

EXAMINATION RESULTS are studied intently by African, Indian and Colored medical students at Natal Medical School. Natal graduates an average of 15 nonwhite doctors each year.

BLOWING OFF STEAM, Africans relieve their frustrations singing and dancing in a Pimville "club"

DANCING THE TWIST, Caroline Moahi, a singer, responds to her partner's steps in the cramped interior of a drinking club in Pimville. The club occupies a room in a private house.

LAUGHING UPROARIOUSLY, a guest at the club finishes a comic song *(right)*. African townships have barnlike municipal beer halls, but many Africans prefer small afterhours clubs.

BELTING OUT A BALLAD, Caroline Moahi spreads her arms wide *(below)*. Miss Moahi sings with a popular Pimville jazz band and had a part in *King Kong*, an all-African musical.

LION
LAGER

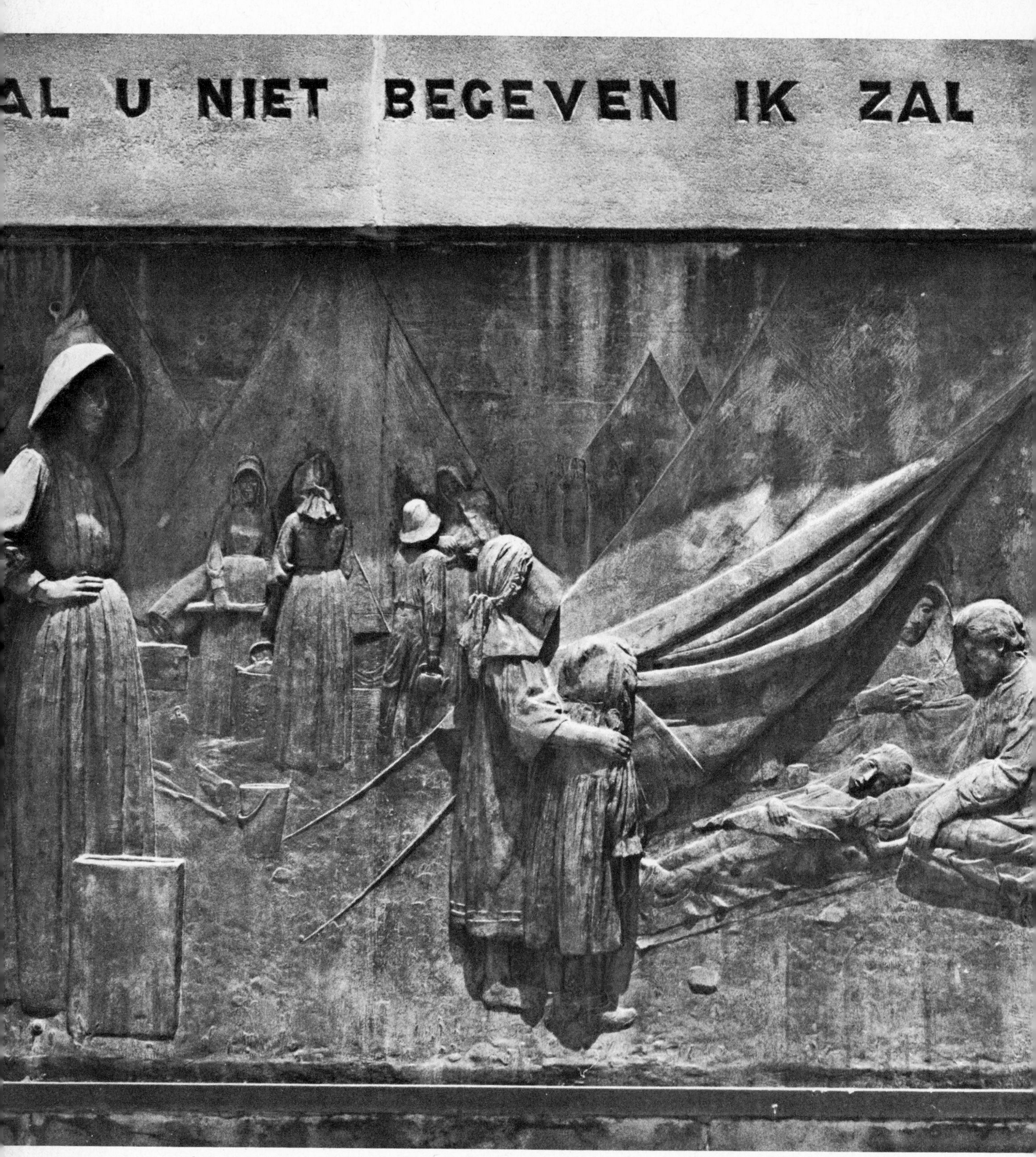

Below an inscription saying "You will never be forgotten or forsaken," a frieze in the Women's Monument outside Bloemfontein depicts a

child dying in a British concentration camp during the Boer War.

The Religion of the Elect

SOUTH AFRICA contains a higher percentage of Christians than any other country on the African continent. A dominating position is held by the three distinct but closely allied Dutch Reformed Churches, to which almost all leading Afrikaners belong. No clear understanding of the country's situation can be gained unless one appreciates something of the organization of these churches, and unless one has formed some picture of the Calvinist faith as Afrikaners understand and accept it, since it is from Calvinism that Afrikaner Nationalism derives its philosophy, its inspiration and its granite resistance to the pattern of world change.

The basic fact is that in South Africa, church and state, religious authority and political power are united to a degree almost unknown in the modern world. And this holds true although the official tie between church and state was severed as far back as 1843. Almost all members of the Cabinet belong to one or other of the Dutch Reformed Churches, together with more than 95 per cent of Nationalist members of Parliament. Dr. Daniel F. Malan, the first

Nationalist Prime Minister when the party came to power in 1948, had himself been a minister, or *predikant,* of the Church. Dr. Malan expressed the attitude of his people and of his church when he said: "The history of the Afrikaner reveals a determination and a definiteness of purpose which makes one feel that Afrikanerdom is not the work of man but a creation of God. Our history is the highest work of art of the architect of the centuries."

Not only does the overwhelming majority of Nationalist politicians belong to one or other of the Dutch Reformed Churches, but also the great majority of Dutch Reformed *predikants* are politically associated with the Nationalist Party. A startlingly large proportion, indeed, belong to the powerful Afrikaner secret society called the Broederbond, which is the very nucleus of Afrikaner Nationalism (see Chapter 9). A recent petition framed by members of one of the three churches made the disclosure that "more than half of the *predikants* of our Gereformeerde Kerk are members of the Broederbond."

The Dutch Reformed Churches, as their name implies, draw their origin and inspiration from Holland, but it is the Holland of the 17th Century, not that of today. The mother church in Holland has been affected by the great tides of liberalism and humanitarianism which have been sweeping over the world for 200 years. The churches in South Africa, however, cut off almost until the end of the 19th Century from any free and regular exchange with the centers of Western thought, have maintained the stern and uncompromising dogmas characteristic of militant Protestantism during the Reformation, four centuries ago.

THE term "Dutch Reformed Church" covers three main groupings: the Nederduitse Gereformeerde Kerk (known by its initials, N.G.K.); the Nederduits Hervormde Kerk (N.H.K.); and the Gereformeerde Kerk. As their names suggest, all three are closely related. Together they claim something like 50 per cent of the three million-odd whites in South Africa.

The N.G.K. is by far the largest. According to the census of 1960, it then included over 1,107,000 whites, 291,000 Coloreds and 297,000 Africans, the Coloreds and Africans being organized into separate units from the whites. Much smaller is the Nederduits Hervormde Kerk, which was the original state church of the Transvaal, and which has continued to look to Holland rather than the Cape for its ministers and spiritual associations. In the 1960 census it claimed about 183,000 white adherents and 30,000 nonwhites.

Smallest of the three is the Gereformeerde Kerk, familiarly known as the Dopper Church, with a total membership of 144,000. This Church was established in 1859, when a group of members seceded from the N.G.K. Strongly fundamentalist in teaching, it is also abnormally strict in its way of life. Dancing, drinking, card-playing, smoking and theatergoing are all frowned upon. It should be added that the Dopper Church is not unique in its opposition to what the world generally regards as harmless pleasures. During their 1963 campaign for "keeping Sunday holy," the three Dutch Reformed Churches all demanded a ban on public swimming, dancing and various other recreations on Sunday, and the Reverend Daniel de Beer, the N.G.K.'s Secretary for Public Morals, added that South African aircraft should not be allowed to leave the country on the Sabbath.

THE wholehearted support given to Nationalist policies by the Dutch Reformed Churches, and particularly their acceptance of apartheid, runs directly counter to Christianity as understood by the outside world. The English-speaking churches in South Africa have expressed themselves strongly on the other side of this issue. The Most Reverend Denis Hurley, Archbishop of Durban, and long the Catholic Church's most outspoken voice in South Africa, said lately: "Apartheid's evil is its refusal of recognition to human dignity," and to fight it is "the challenge of every Christian worthy of the name." Although in some English-speaking churches practice is not always fully in accord with these lofty principles, Protestants and Roman Catholics alike regard racial discrimination as being opposed to the Christian ethic. The Afrikaner churches, on the other hand, regard discrimination as part of their Christianity. To appreciate how the Afrikaners are able to take this standpoint, it is necessary to understand a little of the basic doctrines of Calvinism.

Those who are chiefly credited with working out the pattern of religious thought which is known as

"Calvinism" are two 16th Century churchmen, the Swiss Ulrich Zwingli and the Frenchman John Calvin. Basic to their religious philosophy was the doctrine of predestination. This doctrine, in part a reaction against contemporary abuses of the Roman Catholic Church, denies that salvation can ever be gained by "works"—that is, by anything man himself can achieve in the way of righteousness and goodness. Salvation is the gift of God, which He gives to whomever He wills. Those whom God has chosen are "the elect," predestined to salvation from all eternity, just as the rest—and by far the larger part—of mankind is predestined to eternal damnation.

"Man," wrote Calvin, "is utterly corrupt and depraved, and humility alone becomes him in the presence of God. . . ." Man can best promote God's glory by unquestioning obedience to His will, which is revealed finally and explicitly in the Bible. The Bible is God's word from beginning to end, and is equally authoritative in all its parts.

IT will be seen that though Calvin was in revolt against one absolute authority—that of the Roman Catholic Church—he was engaged in setting up another absolute authority, the Bible, and a new Church to hand down Biblical interpretations. Membership in this new church of the "elect," Calvin preached, was necessary if a man hoped to be saved. God saves no one apart from Christ, and for those not in the church, "there can be no hope of remission of sins nor any salvation."

Such doctrines, which elsewhere in the world have served their day and been softened or modified, have been preserved in the Dutch Reformed Churches of South Africa in almost the full vigor of their birth. When Professor J. J. Muller of the Stellenbosch Theological Seminary was questioned once on whether "a person embracing the Jewish faith can go to heaven like Moses or Elijah," the professor firmly ruled out this possibility. "For Jew and heathen the same demand is put by the Gospel. No one goes to the Father except through Jesus Christ."

It follows then that the true church is a body apart, composed of the elect. The task of the elect is not to serve mankind, or to seek to establish the law of love throughout the world. It is to obey God's commands, and to preserve themselves uncontaminated during their progress through a sinful world. Strong discipline is needed to prevent the weaker brethren from yielding to temptation; this discipline resides in the officers of the church, to whose authority all members must submit.

From this brief review of a few key doctrines, it is clear that the tendency of traditional Calvinism is antidemocratic and authoritarian. It is an exclusive religion. Those who are not of the inner few are outcasts, doomed from the beginning of time. The worst crime of which the elect can be guilty is to consent to the leveling of distinctions and the removal of differences. On the contrary, like the Children of Israel in their wanderings, they ought rather to create new points of difference for the purpose of maintaining separation. To accept those outside the fold as equals is to betray the special position allotted by God only to his chosen.

God is not therefore to be thought of as a uniter, bringing the peoples of the world together. Far from it. God is, in the words of an article in *Die Kerkbode,* the official organ of the N.G.K., "the great Divider," who "found it good to establish boundaries between people and groups of people." "We believe," the article continued, "that white and nonwhite in South Africa, in the light of different cultural peculiarities, psychological differences, biological differences and difference in political aspiration as well as group affiliation, stand under different laws of life."

FROM this position a number of conclusions follow which prove decisive in the political field. First, of course, is the separation of races. Besides supporting political and social apartheid, the Afrikaner churches all maintain separate buildings and organizations for the different racial groups. The second consequence is that compromise is impossible, since that would imply that those who are wholly in the right accept a certain proportion of what is wrong. Liberalism and humanitarianism, for instance, are not regarded as points of view with which one may agree or disagree intellectually. They are deadly and subversive doctrines. And since their theories imply that works, not faith, are required—and even that man can achieve some degree of salvation here on earth by establishing a better way of life open to all human beings—they run directly counter to the expressed will of God. At the 34th General Synod of the Dopper Church in 1961, it was agreed that all false aspirations for unity as preached by liberalism and Communism must be rejected as anti-Christian.

A third consequence flowing from these doctrines is that since compromise is unacceptable, there is little point in discussion. A man of good will should attempt to convert his opponent, but he need not waste time listening to the other person's mistaken arguments. Typical was the action of Dr. Verwoerd, who when Prime Minister would readily give up a couple of hours to explaining his own point of view, but who would cut the interview short at once if counterarguments were advanced.

Fourth, change of any kind is difficult to justify. God has expressed His will once and for all time in the Bible. To accept the need for new interpretations of the Bible and thus for new attitudes toward life is, by implication, to convict the past of error and wrongdoing. But how is it possible for generations of the elect to have been misled? Hence the continual emphasis of the Afrikaners on "traditional policy," and their reverence for what the early Boers and Voortrekkers said and thought, though they were living in a totally different world.

A FIFTH consequence of these doctrines is the belief that everything that happens is a direct expression of the will of God. It occasioned no surprise in Nationalist circles when Dr. Verwoerd, after some extremely tough and bitter in-fighting for the party leadership, declared that it was "God's will" he should become Prime Minister. It is particularly God's will that the Afrikaners should reign over South Africa. This belief was most forcibly expressed by Dr. J. C. Lombard in a church magazine: "The whole of South Africa, from the Cape of Storms to the forest-lined banks of the Limpopo, is God's property which He is lending to us. From the waves that roll onto the east coast to the turbulent waters of the great sea in the west, take possession of it, Afrikaner nation. The Lord wants you to reign over it."

Lastly, a special intensity of hostility is directed by the faithful against Afrikaners who do not conform to the general pattern. Besides being political rebels, they are flouting church authority and defying God's will. Moreover, the disobedience of a few could provoke God's indignation against a whole people, as it did in Old Testament days. Dr. Ben Marais, professor of the history of Christianity at Pretoria University, is one of a small group of dissidents who have suffered heavily for daring to be independent. Writing in an Afrikaans monthly newspaper in March 1961, he quoted as typical the denunciation voiced by an Afrikaner cultural leader: "The greatest sin which an Afrikaner can commit is to be nonconformist."

TO the outsider, a surprising feature of these Calvinist convictions is the way they are made to yield support for aspects of Government policy which would appear to have small connection with religion. To take only two examples: the refusal of the vote to any except whites, and opposition to the United Nations. On both these points church opinion is set out most clearly in a pamphlet, "The Fundamental Principles of Calvinist Christian Political Science," published in 1951 by the Council of the N.G.K., which "earnestly recommends it to the political leaders of our people." On the question of the vote, it says: "The primitive and immature person can be content with passive participation and can but bow humbly because his level of civilization does not justify any voting right. . . . In this regard our greatest problem in South Africa is the viewpoint of revolutionary democracy of the school of Rousseau . . . [according to which] everybody, in our case white and non-white, must have the franchise. . . . As a result, the God-given authority structure of the state is turned upside down, with subject on top and ruler below. In this way the franchise becomes the fantasy of sovereignty opposed to God."

The pamphlet goes on to say that since the African enjoys the protection of the law, "It is thus definitely nonsense to state that the non-white in our fatherland is oppressed when the franchise is withheld from him. . . . The franchise is a trust, granted only to those who have arrived at maturity and can use it with responsibility towards God—the native does not fulfil this requirement, and therefore could not exercise this right correctly. We do not even give our immature children the franchise, and are they therefore slaves?" On such slender arguments as these, the Afrikaner is able to convince himself that it is

"God's will" that the black man should not vote in South African elections.

The futility of the United Nations is a favorite topic with Nationalist politicians, who claim that this body, which has become increasingly critical of South African policies, is doomed to speedy collapse through its own discords and through the multiplicity of unequal nations and races associating there upon equal terms. Their arguments find eager support in the same pamphlet. It explains why not merely U.N., but *all* such attempts to organize world cooperation, are doomed before they start.

Arguing that all state authority is ruling power over subjects *within a specified territory,* it continues: "Purely from this angle we must reject the Humanist ideal of a world-government with a world-state and police or army. The only world power of which the Scriptures teach us in this connection, is that of Anti-Christ, an imperialist and tyrant above all, without any regard for national or state boundaries. . . . The struggle to obliterate national frontiers is thus diabolical. In essence, it strives after the solution of international problems through the medium of an earthly kingdom, and thereby flouts the Scriptural truth that only the Kingdom of Heaven can guarantee peace."

In other words, because 2,000 years ago the only known attempt at a world order was the power of Rome—described by the early Christians as "anti-Christ"—it is today "diabolical" to try and modify national feeling, or to unite across frontiers in the manner now being carried out in Europe (and long ago in the United States). The pamphlet ends with a breathtaking inversion of the Christian message of peace, saying that such attempts to abolish war are a "flouting" of "Scriptural truth."

THE foregoing will perhaps explain how it is that a devoutly Christian people, the Afrikaners, have markedly increased, rather than decreased, the amount of discrimination during their years of rule in South Africa. A brief flare-up of moderate opinion did take place in 1960. This was the year of the "Cottesloe Conference" of the World Council of Churches held in Johannesburg, at which representatives of the Dutch Reformed Churches were present. A number of "liberal" resolutions were passed, including one declaring that "no one who believes in Christ should be excluded from any church on grounds of his color or race." Representatives of two of the three Dutch Reformed Churches supported this resolution. The third strongly dissented. But when the Government stamped its foot, the delegates were sharply disowned by their own synods and the flare-up rapidly died down. Later, however, there came into being the Christian Institute. Headed by a stout-hearted and enlightened predikant, the Reverend Mr. Beyers Naudé, it opposed religious apartheid. Also, a Dutch Reformed Church commission criticized as "a moral cancer" the effects of apartheid on African family life.

ANYONE who has studied the racial attitudes of the Dutch Reformed Churches will not be surprised that though they include almost twice as many whites as all the other Protestant churches in South Africa, these other churches contain nine times as many Africans and almost twice as many Coloreds as the Afrikaner churches. The Methodist Church has a particularly strong hold on the African; it has more black clergy ordained than white, and almost five times as many black members of congregations.

More serious, however, than their choice of one church rather than another is the fact that great numbers of Africans are turning away from Christianity altogether, regarding it as the "religion of apartheid." As former Cabinet Minister Harry Lawrence reported to the South African Parliament in 1960, the Africans have told their clergymen "that they were prepared to forsake Western Christianity because there was no truth in it. 'Before the white men came to South Africa, we had our own religion and our own gods and we are now going back to them.'" Many Africans, in fact, are becoming Moslems. Islam has no color bar; it has no association with the exploiting white man; and it allows a man to have more than one wife, in a society where a wife can be a valuable economic asset.

A few years before he left South Africa, the former Anglican Archbishop of Cape Town, Joost de Blank, declared: "If the churches in South Africa live up to the teaching of the Gospel, the Africans may listen to them. But if they come to be identified with the ruling clique, the Africans will turn against them." That is exactly what is happening now.

At a missionary outpost called Tshilidzini in the Transvaal, a white minister conducts services for a congregation of Africans.

A Firm Stand Based on Strong Moral Convictions

An outside observer of South African life might assume that the dominating Afrikaner policies and attitudes derive from a spirit of cynicism and self-aggrandizement. However, the Afrikaner does not see matters in this light at all. Far from sensing that he is oppressing the Africans, the Afrikaner believes that white domination is the only possible means of saving white civilization in the country. Cut off from the liberalizing currents of European thought during the last two centuries, condemned by the world and isolated in a predominantly black continent, he doggedly maintains his stringent Calvinism and his moral convictions. Self-righteous and loyal to his pioneer traditions, he applies his values to every area of life, from missionary work with the natives, shown here, to athletic endeavor *(next pages)*.

TEACHING a class of women of the Venda tribe to read their native language, a missionary of the Dutch Reformed Church encourages tribal traditions at Tshilidzini (Place of Grace).

EXAMINING a Venda woman who is suffering from pellagra, a malnutrition disease *(below)*, a doctor at the Tshilidzini mission's hospital for chronic illnesses listens to her breathing.

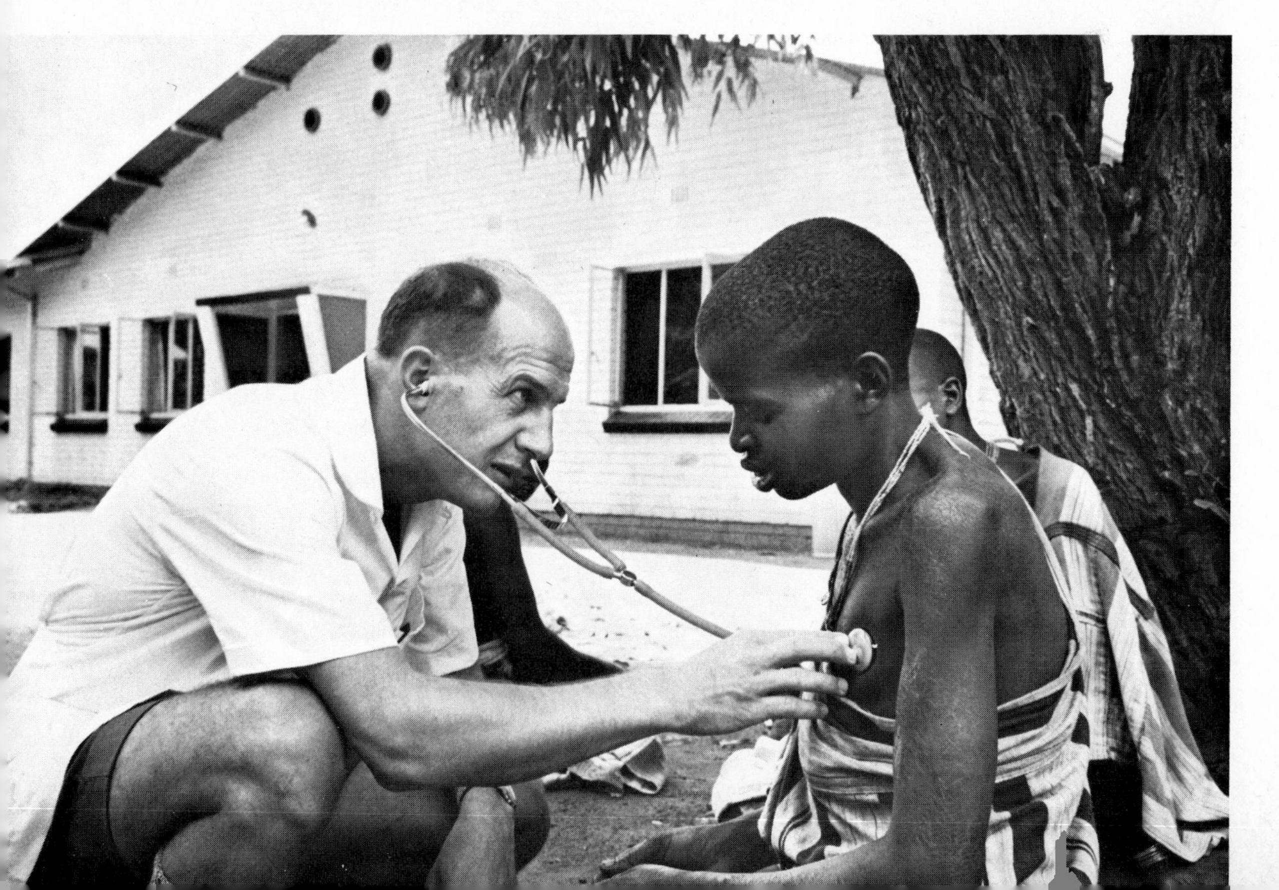

HIGH FLIGHT is taken by a girl as Afrikaners toss her on a blanket during celebrations of the Day of the Covenant in Pretoria. In the background is the imposing Voortrekker Monument, which commemorates the Great Trek of 1836-1838.

PRECISION DRILL of young Afrikaner gymnasts *(right)* unfolds in the Pretoria amphitheater on the Day of the Covenant. Afrikaner zealots take these nationalistic spectacles seriously, and are dismayed that attendance has fallen in recent years.

SMART SALUTE greets an official as two "Voortrekker" scouts snap to attention on the Day of the Covenant. The Voortrekker movement was founded by Afrikaners who disliked the interracial policies of the international Scout organization.

PATRIOTIC FERVOR animates the mass observance of an Afrikaner holiday

Novelist Alan Paton, best known for "Cry, the Beloved Country," looks out over a valley in Natal. He has written about the sufferings

of the Africans and headed the now disbanded Liberal Party.

A Search for Truth in the Arts

THE cultural life of South Africa is a tragic fragmentation. There is so much ability and already considerable achievement, but work which should be acclaimed by all, challenging and stimulating writers and artists over the whole country, is confined within narrow walls of race and color. There have been African writers, musicians and sculptors whose work would deserve to be judged by the highest contemporary standards; but they have been largely cut off from the teaching they need, from contact with other artists facing similar problems and from the collective achievement of the past.

On the other side of the fence there are white short-story writers and novelists writing about the life of black men and women with no firsthand knowledge and little contact, piecing impressions together from what they hear or from what they are told by their servants. They *want* to know. They would rather write out of knowledge than out of guesswork, but they find themselves unable to get past the official barriers or past those unofficial barriers of distrust and doubt which have grown around and out of the official ones. Afrikaans-speaking, English-speaking and African writers and artists are isolated from one another by the country's social, political and linguistic barriers. And over all contemporary work hangs the dead hand of censorship—a dead hand which is very much alive when it fastens upon its victims. You can be safe, of course, quite easily. Avoid dealing with sex, religion, politics and the racial question—but what then will you write about, and what relevance will it have to the ever more tense situation in which you, as a South African writer or artist, have to live?

CENSORSHIP deals most roughly with the printed word, of course, since the statement made in this form is usually obvious and explicit. But it is in literature, despite isolation and censorship, that South Africans have made their most distinctive contributions to the arts. It is impossible in a single chapter to examine in detail the work, past and present, of three separate groups of writers, but even a brief survey reveals a remarkable achievement.

Of the three main cultural groups, the writers in English are the most favorably placed. Though the market in South Africa is small, it is extremely active. In addition, the worldwide interest in South Africa has opened up a big overseas market, especially in the English-speaking countries.

The writing of novels in English about South Africa began in earnest in 1883 with the appearance of a classic, Olive Schreiner's *The Story of an African Farm.* Though Olive Schreiner, sister of the Cape politician who cooperated with Cecil Rhodes, wrote other books (notably *Trooper Peter Halket of Mashonaland,* an attack on Rhodes's empire-building), she never regained that early level, and it was not until the 1920s that novels of South African life began to take a place on the world's literary scene.

Among the new writers were Sarah Gertrude Millin, William Plomer and Ethelreda Lewis. Mrs. Millin's best-known book, *God's Stepchildren,* appeared in 1924. Her theme was the disastrous results of miscegenation, which she traced down through four haunted and doomed generations. Today's readers may feel that the tragic fate which destroys her racially mixed characters comes rather from the author's attitude than from their own natures, but Mrs. Millin was among the first to write of Colored people and open up the present vein of interest in the life of the nonwhites.

William Plomer was one of the first to write of the African, and to write of him not as if he were just part of the picturesque South African scene but as an individual with his own separate life and problems. Plomer was still in his early twenties when *Turbott Wolfe,* his first novel, was published in 1925. Plomer left the country the next year, but has since often harked back to it. In his collection of short stories, *Four Countries,* he allotted one section to South Africa. It includes "Ula Masondo," in which the plot—black man coming up from the Reserves to work in the mines and encountering city life—sets a pattern which would be followed by writers many times over in the next decades.

Ethelreda Lewis, who is probably best known for the *Trader Horn* books, also wrote of the African. Her novel *Mantis* (1926) deals with the impact of Western civilization on tribal life—another vein which would be determinedly exploited by others.

ASSOCIATED with William Plomer in the '20s was Laurens van der Post, another writer who has since achieved a worldwide reputation. His first novel, *In a Province,* is again the tale of a simple child of nature involved in city life. In 1926, Plomer, Van der Post and the poet Roy Campbell launched the monthly magazine *Voorslag* (Whiplash). Its aim, as later defined by Plomer, was "to sting with satire the mental hindquarters . . . of the bovine citizenry of the Union." Though it lasted only for two or three numbers—after which Campbell resigned and Plomer and Van der Post left the country—the sting stayed in the wound and is still remembered.

Campbell—the outstanding South African poet who has written in English—also exiled himself from South Africa. A flamboyant figure, he never received the appreciation his work deserves, largely because his prejudices—being aristocratic and authoritarian—ran counter to those of the age in which he lived. Despite this, however, his work has had a strong influence on the poets who followed, including Roy Macnab, Guy Butler and Anthony Delius. Campbell's first major work, *The Flaming Terrapin,* a long poem based on the Flood, not only made audible a new poetic voice but introduced a critic who had set himself to transform the nature of South African writing. He failed in this, as was inevitable, and his next work, "The Wayzgoose" (1928), showed his contempt for a people too absorbed in politics and money-making to respond:

Attend my fable if your ears be clean,
In fair Banana Land we lay our scene—
South Africa, renowned both far and wide
For politics and little else beside:
Where, having torn the land with shot and shell,
Our sturdy pioneers as farmers dwell,
And, 'twixt the hours of strenuous sleep, relax
To shear the fleeces, or to fleece the blacks.

In 1927 Campbell went to England, then to the south of France, afterward taking part in the Spanish Civil War on Franco's side. His later works include *Adamastor* (1930), in which some of his finest lyrics appear.

Another whose work aroused powerful reactions in South Africa was the novelist Stuart Cloete, whose *Turning Wheels* appeared in 1937. In *Turning Wheels* he attempted to treat with realism Afrikanerdom's most cherished subject of romance, the Great Trek. The attempt, in particular Cloete's picture of the rough-and-ready sexual behavior of some of the characters, was bitterly resented as a slight upon heroic ancestors, and the book was banned in South Africa. Cloete has written more than a dozen novels since, and achieved considerable popular success, but his writing has settled down into a formula and *Turning Wheels* remains his most genuine book.

OF the many books published in the 1940s, two in particular survive, one for its worldwide success, the other despite its having been—from a publishing standpoint—a failure. The success was Alan Paton's powerful but sentimental *Cry, the Beloved Country* (1948), which has been called the *Uncle Tom's Cabin* of South Africa, since it is less a work of art than an impassioned plea for understanding of the black man's problems. It was followed by Paton's *Too Late the Phalarope,* which was also widely read in the English-speaking world, and in 1961 by his collection of short stories, *Tales from a Troubled Land,* in which detachment touched with humor has replaced the author's early striving for emotional effects.

The other most remarkable book of the 1940s is a volume of short stories by Herman Bosman called *Mafeking Road,* which records with tender insight and delightful humor the life of an Afrikaner farming community in the Transvaal in the early years of this century. Unknown outside South Africa—and far too little known inside—it is one of those books which is biding its time and will certainly achieve recognition one day. Bosman's life was disturbed and tragic, but before his early death he completed an autobiographical novel of prison life whose grimness is reflected in its title, *Cold Stone Jug.*

THE 1950s brought a crop of new writers, notably Nadine Gordimer, whose stories are widely known in America from their publication in *The New Yorker* magazine. Miss Gordimer has written several novels dealing with the South African scene, but her most distinctive work is found in her two short-story collections, *Six Feet of the Country* (1956) and *The Soft Voice of the Serpent* (1957). In her stories Miss Gordimer often examines with honesty and delicate psychological insight the difficulties of blacks and whites in their attempts to understand and communicate with one another.

Dan Jacobson, a young Jewish writer born in Johannesburg, achieved early success with *A Dance in the Sun* (1956). He now lives in London and already has half a dozen books to his credit. Other prose writers whose work has made a mark are Harry Bloom, Anthony Delius, Daphne Rooke, Sylvester Stein, Lewis Sowden and James Ambrose Brown.

Afrikaans is a language of great simplicity and force. Derived from 17th and 18th Century rather than from present-day Dutch, it is a bony language lending itself well to poetry, to descriptions of the South African landscape, and to a harsh symbolism. Afrikaner intellectuals—largely clergy, professors, educators and political journalists—cherish the same feeling about their language as they do about their race. It must be kept "pure" from foreign words and expressions. On the popular level, however, a steady incorporation of foreign words goes on, so that there is a considerable difference between the language written by the intellectuals and that commonly spoken, especially in the cities.

An equally wide gulf also exists between the work that is praised by the critics and that which is read by the mass of the people. The books the average Afrikaner reads are, not surprisingly, of the *skiet en donder* (blood and thunder) type, hundreds of which are published every year. In addition there is a lavish production of cheap sex fiction, bitterly ranted against from platform and pulpit. One result of this split in taste is that for the serious creative writer in Afrikaans, almost the only hope of earning more than pocket money is for a book to be chosen for use in schools. But to be so chosen it must first pass through a filter of school boards and educational authorities.

OUTRAGED Afrikaner comment flared up over the publication a few years ago of Jan Rabie's *Ons, die Afgod* (We, the False God), though Rabie attempted no more than a realistic treatment of white-Colored relations. Etienne le Roux's *Die Mugu* raised another indignant dust storm, but for a different reason—his book was concerned with Afrikaner "ducktails" (juvenile delinquents). Frans Venter's *Die Swart Pelgrim* (translated in 1959 under the title *Dark Pilgrim)* handled its time-honored subject—the black man coming to town—in a benevolent, paternalistic way, and therefore aroused mainly benevolent reactions. These three, with Uys Krige, who writes equally well in English and Afrikaans, are the four chief contemporary prose writers. Their task, difficult enough before, was made immensely harder by the censorship act of 1963. Lately, however, a movement known as *Sestiger* (men of the sixties) has demanded the right to treat problems of present-day South Africa more openly and frankly. This modern spirit has even found support in the *Akademie,* the cultural power center of the Afrikaner people.

Of earlier prose writers, C. M. van den Heever, Jochem van Bruggen, Mikro (the pen name of C. H. Kuhn) and D. F. Malherbe are probably the best known. Deneys Reitz wrote his outstanding sketchbook of the Boer War, *Commando* (1929), in English. Eugene Marais' admirable study, *The Soul of the White Ant,* appeared first in Afrikaans and later (1937) in English.

However, it is in poetry that the mainstream of Afrikaans writing is to be traced, and for this there is both an emotional and a practical reason. Deeply involved in the life of the country he so largely developed, the Afrikaner turns naturally to poetry for the expression of his feelings. At the same time, in a country where criticism is so bitterly resented, poetry offers a safer outlet. Dealing in metaphor and allusion, the poet expresses himself less directly, and therefore with less risk.

It was thus possible for the Colored poet S. V. Petersen not only to write the following short poem "Conclusion" (here given in translation), but to see it included in the *Groot Verseboek* (Big Book of Verse), the national anthology prescribed for school reading throughout the country.

Blond hair and fair skin,
Can they take crown and scepter too in death?
(The pallbearers pace to a death march)
And darkness waits for you, for me, for both of us.

In the early days—that is, around the turn of the century—the task the poets set themselves was a double one. They were helping to develop the new language and also seeking to formulate the background of the *volk* in a dramatic and memorable form. A poet who called himself Totius (based on his real name, J. D. du Toit) was a professor of theology who wrote long, somber epics relating the sufferings of the Boer people to those of the children of Israel. His publication dates are mainly between 1912 and 1937, when his complete rhymed version of the Psalms in Afrikaans appeared. C. Louis Leipoldt (1880-1947) wrote about the Boer War, and like his contemporary Jan Celliers also wrote much nature poetry.

HOWEVER, it is in the present-day poets that Afrikaans literature finds its full strength, and it is a tragedy that, working in isolation, they have had so little work adequately translated and recognized abroad. Some judges say that poets such as N. P. van Wyk Louw (pronounced Fun Veyk Low), D. J. Opperman and Elizabeth Eybers could be poets of world stature if their writing were sufficiently known. Van Wyk Louw is the most admired poet writing in Afrikaans today; his best-known works include *Raka,* a long epic about an imaginary tribe with a mystical belief in a figure, half-human and half-animal, and his verse drama *Germanicus*. Opperman is a poet of power and feeling who refuses to confine himself to patriotic or nature poetry.

The earliest African writers used their own tribal languages, and although the African population as a whole did not start to become literate much before 1910, there was African writing, largely missionary-inspired, 40 years before. A convenient starting date for anything other than religious verse and moral anecdote would be 1884, with the founding of the paper *Imvo Zabantsunde* (African Opinion). The contrast between the professions of Christianity and the white man's practice—a shock still deeply felt all over Africa—was a common theme, treated at times with surprising sophistication. A second was the strain felt by the Africans in adapting themselves to the demands of industry. The glories of the heroic past also inspired many African writers. In the first decades of this century, remarkable work was done by Thomas Mofolo in the Sesotho language, by Mqhayi in Xhosa and by Moses Mphahlele and H.I.E. Dhlomo in English. Mofolo's fine historical romance, *Chaka,* based on the life of the great Zulu warrior and tyrant, resembles in its theme Shakespeare's *Macbeth.* Chaka is told by supernatural forces that he can become ruler on a far greater scale than he has ever dreamed of, but that the pathway to power lies through blood. Chaka kills his beloved, Noliwe, and leads the Zulu people to lordship over much of southern Africa. At the height of his power, Chaka is plagued by nightmares in which those he has betrayed appear to haunt him. Finally he is murdered by his brothers, and even the hyenas do not touch his corpse.

In 1930 appeared *Mhudi,* Sol Plaatje's historical romance built round another great African hero, Mzilikazi, one of Chaka's generals, who founded a separate kingdom for himself. Plaatje, who wrote in English as well as his native language, was an early member of the African National Congress. Although, like Mofolo, he celebrated in his writing the heroic past of his people, he was in his own life an active political organizer who looked to the future. For example, he rode a bicycle from farm to farm trying to organize the squatters who had been driven off "white" farms following the Land Act of 1913.

The most notable writer in the first half of the 20th Century, however, was the poet B. W. Vilakazi, a Zulu from Natal. Vilakazi, born in 1906, was appointed to the Department of Bantu Studies at the University of the Witwatersrand, becoming the first African ever to teach at a South African "white" university. This was in 1936. Ten years later his university made him a Doctor of Literature, again the first African to achieve this distinction. He died the next year at the age of 41.

When we come to the present day, the main current of African writing runs through short stories—stories which often read like autobiography—and autobiographical writing with the drama and intensity of fiction. A group of writers working in these forms has centered around the Johannesburg magazine *Drum,* either as members of the staff—like Ezekiel Mphahlele, Casey Motsisi, Bloke Modisane, Arthur Maimane and the late Todd Matshikiza and Can Themba—or else like Dyke Sentso, Peter Clark (also known as "Peter Kumalo") and Richard Rive, who had their early work published through the magazine. Some of these same writers, both African and Colored, have also contributed to the literary magazine called *The Classic,* edited by a former *Drum* reporter, the late Nathaniel Nakasa.

All of these men have worked in English, partly because their writing has been aimed at the outside world and partly because for an African under modern conditions, the use of English is a form of protest. Between them they have helped to build up a new

JOYOUS MUSIC IN THE STREETS

Sidewalk bands, often made up of tiny children, abound in the streets of African cities and townships. The most common melodic instrument is the penny whistle, which is made of simple metal tubing a half inch in diameter. The tube, about 14 inches long, is flattened at one end to form a mouthpiece and is drilled with six finger holes. Shrill and limited in range, the penny whistle nevertheless can be made to produce some very hot jazz in the hands of a virtuoso. The most celebrated penny whistler in South Africa is Lemmie ("Special") Mabaso, who began playing for pennies on the streets of Johannesburg at the age of seven, and 10 years later was making best-selling records and playing in stage appearances. Later on Mabaso also became expert on the saxophone.

culture, a culture of the city, which neither harks back to the heroes of the past nor longs for a vanished simplicity. Under normal conditions one could expect their work before long to blend in with that of white writers to produce a body of South African literature in which all that would matter would be the quality of the individual's contribution, and the color of his skin could be forgotten. As it is, however, they must find readers mainly among their own people, or else overseas.

WHEN one turns to drama, it would require an afflatus of patriotic fervor to take seriously either South Africa's theater or film industry. Johannesburg, Cape Town and Pretoria all possess imposing theater buildings, but they are used mainly for short runs of successful importations from London or Broadway. The outstanding event of recent years was the African musical *King Kong,* which had a book by Harry Bloom and music by Todd Matshikiza.

In music, as in poetry, the Afrikaners are far ahead of the English-speaking, but here too there is a split between the music praised by critics and that which is popularly enjoyed. There are five outstanding composers, all Afrikaans-speaking: Arnold van Wyk, Hubert du Plessis, Stefans Grové, John Joubert and Gideon Fagan. But in spite of the support given them by the South African Broadcasting Corporation, they receive almost no popular recognition. The corporation presents their stark, difficult music on patriotic occasions. But on the popular programs it is the basic, monotonous beat of *boeremusiek*—a kind of hillbilly music—hour after hour.

Much nearer the idiom of the present day is the popular music of the Africans. The only composer known outside the country is Todd Matshikiza, but a number of instrumentalists are familiar from their recordings of jazz and *kwela,* the latter based on the instrument popularly called the "penny whistle." The rich voice and delightful personality of Miriam Makeba have made Xhosa and Zulu folk songs familiar to millions in America and Europe.

Before 1900 the only painting of any account done in South Africa was the work of two talented but conventional English artists, Thomas Bowler and Thomas Baines. They were succeeded by popular painters of the "sunset on the plains" school, such as Hugo Naudé, W. J. Volschenk, W. H. Coertzer, Gwelo Goodman and Gabriel de Jongh, who flourished on into World War II. Their style of painting is still the most popular, hundreds of copies or near variations being turned out in Johannesburg back streets to be hawked across the platteland of the Free State and Transvaal.

New life was introduced into South African painting in the 1920s when Maggie Laubser and Irma Stern brought the new Expressionism back from Germany; and in 1938 came the formation of the "New Group," under the leadership of Gregoire Boonzaier. Today, the most highly esteemed artists are Alexis Preller, who has evolved a strange personal mythology from the varied settings of African life; Walter Battiss, whose careful study of Bushman rock paintings is reflected in his work; Gordon Vorster, with his vivid, abstract studies of wildlife; Maud Sumner; Cecil Higgs; Bettie Cilliers-Barnard and Rupert Shephard. Among Africans, the painting of pictures as an art form has made no great headway. Gerard Sekoto, who went to Paris in the late 1940s, has achieved the dignity of a one-man exhibition. Peter Clark (also known as a writer) has begun to establish himself in Cape Town and Johannesburg.

Of sculptors the best-known names are Hennie Potgieter, Coert Steynberg, Lippy Lipshitz, Moses Kottler and Edoardo Villa. But the most interesting work in this field is being done by two Africans, Lucas Sithole and Sidney Kumalo. Kumalo has also done striking studies in charcoal.

FOR a few Africans and Coloreds in the fields of art and writing, creative ability may open doors and bring contacts with other races as well as with the world outside. But for most, the opportunities of breaking down the barriers are few and far between. So we return to the point where we began—the tragic fragmentation, for political, racial and linguistic reasons, of South Africa's whole artistic life. This is accentuated by the deep cleavage of taste—particularly among Afrikaners—between what is critically approved and what is bought, read, listened to, or looked at. Were it not for these divisions—and for restrictions in the form of censorship, official and unofficial—the vigor of creative effort coming from this small country might well astonish the world.

South Africa's foremost poet, N. P. van Wyk Louw, is the writer most responsible for perfecting Afrikaans as a poetic language.

Artistic Freedom and Government Interference

Personal expression in the arts requires clear vision and the freedom to describe what one sees. In South Africa there are many creative people who are able to view themselves and their society lucidly, but their right to express these insights publicly has been sharply curtailed. Afrikaner writers, whether voluntarily or unwillingly, have generally avoided touching upon inflammatory social questions. They have confined their efforts largely to strong, meditative poetry or to epic accounts of Boer history. English-speaking authors are more outspoken about the suffering in South Africa, but censorship laws make it increasingly difficult for their books to be read. The plastic arts, because they do not present a message or comment as openly as literature, receive less official direction and interference. Nevertheless, the harshness of Government censorship has ironically served to unite South African artists and writers—African, English-speaking and Afrikaner—all of whom are strongly opposed to censorship, whatever their point of view.

CAUSTIC NOVELIST, Nadine Gordimer deals with the complacency and guilt of South Africa's whites in books like *Occasion for Loving*. Her short stories frequently appear in European and American publications.

BOLD CRITIC, D. J. Opperman *(below)*, who writes Afrikaans poetry, aroused furious protest in 1957 with his "Christmas Carol," which describes the birth of a Colored Christ Child in Cape Town's Colored slum.

NEW GRADUATES of the University of Cape Town leave the campus with diplomas *(opposite)*. A 1959 Government act establishing separate universities for nonwhites aroused strong opposition at Cape Town.

CELEBRATED POET, P. J. Philander *(left)*, a Colored who writes in his native language, Afrikaans, has been widely honored for his work. He now devotes his full time to his duties as principal of a Colored high school.

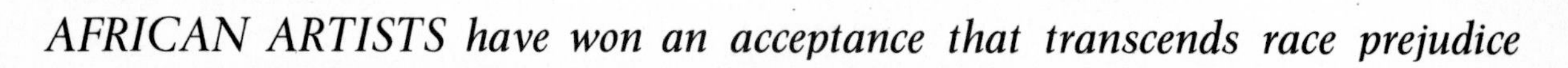

AFRICAN ARTISTS ***have won an acceptance that transcends race prejudice***

RELIGIOUS THEMES and traditional African forms dominate the work of Lucas Sithole, dynamic young African sculptor whose figures are made of wood sheathed in copper. Discriminatory practices do not radically restrict the professional activities of an African artist; Sithole is free to exhibit side-by-side with white artists in an art gallery which is administered by whites.

JAZZ COMPOSER, the late Todd Matshikiza *(right)* wrote the music for the African "jazz opera," *King Kong*, performed in South Africa in 1959. Although the cast was African, the book, lyrics and financing were supplied by whites. The result was a uniquely successful combining of African and Western themes.

FOREMOST SCULPTOR among African artists, Sidney Kumalo stands behind a statue of a dying bull *(below)*. A member of an interracial art movement inspired by African forms and themes, Kumalo has also executed a series of sculptures depicting the Stations of the Cross for a church in the Free State.

Grimly tight-lipped after the assassination of Prime Minister R. H. Verwoerd, leaders of the Nationalist Party surround Verwoerd's

successor, Johannes Vorster, as he reads his acceptance speech in 1966.

9

Politics above and below the Surface

ON the surface, the political life of South Africa is a contest between the Nationalist Party, representing the political ideals of the Afrikaners, and the United Party, representing the interests of the English-speaking people. Since the Afrikaners now have a 60 to 40 majority over the English-speaking, and since they are more politically resolute, the contest becomes more one-sided with each election.

The franchise in South Africa is confined to whites, male and female, over 18 years of age. No Colored, however "near-white," and no African or Asian, however many university degrees he may obtain or whatever his service to the community, is entitled to vote on the common roll. Since the voteless Africans, Asians and Coloreds are multiplying faster than the whites, this means that the country becomes more of an oligarchy and less of a democracy with every passing year.

However, to regard the country's political life as a recurring contest between the Nationalist and the United Parties—in the sense that American political life is a recurring contest between Democrats and

Republicans—would be to misunderstand the forces governing the country's destiny. The true struggle in South Africa is not the apparent one between the two major parties but a three-cornered struggle, waged in part beneath the surface, between Afrikaner nationalism, African nationalism and the economic power of the English-speaking people. In this continuing struggle, the political parties are by no means the only instruments.

THE Nationalist Party is indeed the outward manifestation of the Afrikaner political philosophy. There are many, however, who believe that the philosophy itself is shaped not by the party but in the councils of a smaller and more secretive body, the Afrikaner Broederbond, or "Band of Brothers." Similarly, though the economic power of the English-speaking section of the population provides the United Party's main support, the party is not the only channel through which that power is directed. As for African nationalism, it has been without open expression since a 1960 law banned the main African political organizations. It would be naïve to imagine, however, that it has therefore ceased to exist, or been rendered permanently impotent.

The story of South African politics since the Boer War is essentially one of the growth of Afrikaner power and with it the expansion of the Nationalist Party. Beaten in that war, but hardly reconciled to British rule, many Afrikaners saw in the generous Act of Union (see Chapter 4) an opportunity to recover everything they had lost. With this long-term aim in view, the Nationalist Party was founded in 1912. More moderate parties and their leaders managed, with ever-increasing difficulty, to retain control of the country's policies for the better part of four decades after the Act of Union, but the militant Afrikaners steadily gained power until, in 1948, they finally succeeded in getting what now appears to be a permanent grip on the Government.

To understand the present situation it is necessary to see how this shift in the balance of power came about. South Africa's first Prime Minister after Union had been the Boer general and popular hero, Louis Botha. Botha's policy, like that of his fellow general and successor, Jan Christian Smuts, was to work for a reconciliation of the two white peoples. In time, Botha and Smuts succeeded in winning the support of almost all of the English-speaking South Africans, as well as that of the more moderate of their fellow Afrikaners, for what was called the South African Party.

Trouble, however, was not long in coming. When during World War I Botha and Smuts brought South Africa into the conflict on the side of Great Britain, some of their former military colleagues from the Boer War staged scattered uprisings. A majority of Afrikaners, strongly anti-British and pro-German, sympathized with the rebels. The split between the forces of moderation and the militant Afrikaner nationalists grew wider and wider and many of the previous admirers of Botha and Smuts joined the ranks of the Nationalists.

Botha died in 1919 and was succeeded by Smuts. Less than a year later, in the postwar elections of 1920, the Nationalist Party emerged as the most powerful single force in the country. Smuts continued in power until 1924 by means of an alliance with the "Vote British" Unionist Party, but then the Nationalists gained control of 63 seats in the Parliament, and James Barry Hertzog, founder of the Nationalist Party, became Prime Minister. The power of Hertzog and his party was far from absolute, however, and when in 1933 the economic depression hit South Africa, the Nationalists were forced to form a coalition Government, allying themselves with their opponent, Smuts, to constitute the United Party.

COALITION may be a good way of facing economic difficulties, but to many Nationalists it was simply a return to the old policy of compromise with the English-speaking which they had rejected 20 years before. And it was in reaction to this policy that Dr. Daniel F. Malan, long one of Hertzog's lieutenants, broke away to organize his own "purified Nationalist Party." Thus the stage was set for today's political conflicts between a still more militant Nationalist Party—"purified" of all urge to compromise—and the loosely united group of interests which makes up the ironically named United Party.

In 1939, when World War II broke out, Smuts, opposing his leader Hertzog, was able to swing South Africa into the conflict on Britain's side, but with a Parliamentary majority of only 80 to 67. This time there was no rebellion, as there had been in 1914, but there was a large section of Afrikaner opinion that first counted on, then hoped for and at last bitterly despaired of a German victory. This group included two recent Prime Ministers, Dr. Verwoerd and Johannes Vorster. By the time of the first postwar election, which was held in 1948, accumulated discontents had mounted up. The Nationalists under Daniel F. Malan and the Afrikaner Party, a splinter group led by Nicolaas C. Havenga, joined forces and—to the country's surprise and to the consternation of the United Party—gained the day. Seventy Nationalist candidates and nine of the Afrikaner Party members were elected, resulting in a bare majority of five for the Nationalists. They have managed to increase their party's majority, however, with each succeeding election.

On taking office after the crucial election in 1948, Dr. Malan exclaimed: "Today South Africa belongs to us [the Afrikaners] once more. . . . May God grant that it will always remain our own." The years since then have been devoted by the Nationalists to ensuring that the divine intention should not fail for want of earthly support.

AN impressive mass of legislation has been driven through the House of Assembly. Seldom has the conventional sneer that parliaments are merely "talking-shops" been so little justified. "We have the majority," the Nationalists say in effect, "and we mean to pass these laws. Why raise objections we shall overrule, or propose amendments we shall not accept?" Democracy—to which the Nationalist Party leaders pay lip service—is thought of not as a system of government in which the rights of the individual are cherished and the will of the people as a whole expressed; it is rather a series of forms to be observed and rules to be complied with—or altered if they prove to be inconvenient.

The aim of virtually all of the legislation enacted since 1948 has been that of ensuring the survival of the Afrikaner group. In the particular circumstances in which they are placed, they can survive, they believe, only if they dominate. Their strength lies in their excellent organization as well as in their firm party discipline.

In its organization, the Nationalist Party manages to combine strong central control with a federal structure. Annual congresses are held in all the South African provinces, at which Nationalist Party members can express their feelings, pass resolutions and elect officers to the provincial executive committees. From among the members of these executive committees, much smaller steering committees are chosen that guide and discipline the parties within each province. In addition, each provincial congress nominates seven members to the Federal Council of the Nationalist Party. This body also has its own steering committee, made up of the four provincial leaders. Here lies the real center of power, especially since these provincial leaders are also leading members of the Cabinet. As a result of this odd but extremely neat arrangement, there is no fear of a clash between the party executive and the leaders of the party in Parliament, since the two groups are made up of the same few men.

It is this combination of an extensive provincial framework with a compact power plant at the center of government that enables the Nationalist Party to maintain a strict inner discipline and strong direction and at the same time to allow free speech at the party's outer edges.

Even more than in its ingenious construction, the Nationalist Party's strength lies in its tight hold over individual members. Everyone on joining binds himself by a solemn pledge to carry out all of his obligations under the provincial constitution, and to submit to party discipline, promising his "undivided loyalty." Nor is this a mere form of words. The new member at once becomes part of a group under a group leader, who must make contact with him at least once every three months. Constant activity is kept up during the year—canvassing for new members, distributing party literature, arranging discussions and planning the provincial congresses.

THIS well-organized and disciplined Nationalist Party was led after September 1966 by South Africa's seventh Prime Minister, Johannes Vorster. Vorster was a short, burly man with bright blue eyes under bushy brows, a square face and a set jaw. During World War II he had been an ardent supporter of the German cause, rising to the position of "General" in the Ossewabrandwag, a paramilitary organization that devoted part of its energies to blowing up troop trains and similar acts of sabotage. Until his accession to power, Mr. Vorster was known principally as the Minister of Justice who extended the powers of the special branch police, acquired new authority to ban and deport opponents, transformed the right of 90-day imprisonment without trial into one of 180 days and implemented his country's detention laws ruthlessly. Following his accession to power as Prime Minister, however, he showed himself—compared to his predecessor, Dr. Verwoerd—more concerned with the realities of power and less with the logic of his position. He had a sense of humor, was liked by many of those who met him personally, and was prepared at times to bend the principles of apartheid in the interest of extending his country's influence over its neighbors.

If Vorster was able, as some suggested, to appear as a man of "flexible granite," this was largely because his predecessor was a man of granite pure and simple. Dr. Verwoerd laid down theories of apartheid to which human beings of all colors and races had to conform. Vorster, apartheid's practitioner, allowed himself an occasional modification of principle to make practice more smooth-running or to gain practical advantage for his country. As regards policy, however, Vorster had to live with the legacy he inherited from a man who—though not himself an Afrikaner but a Dutchman by birth—was certainly the ablest and the most extraordinary of all Nationalist Afrikaner politicians.

Dr. Verwoerd's rise in the Nationalist Party had been extremely rapid. Despite his defeat when he first stood for Parliament in 1948, he was soon appointed to a seat in the Senate, and in 1950 he began an eight-year term as Minister of Native Affairs. In this position he showed a capacity to drive his projects through regardless of opposition from inside or outside the party. He was also able to present his policies in a manner that, if not satisfying to the world at large, took careful account of the Afrikaners' moral attitudes and religious susceptibilities. Only 10 years after his electoral defeat in 1948, Dr. Verwoerd was chosen Prime Minister by the Nationalist Party caucus and proceeded to give Nationalist policy an entirely new twist by his creation of the Bantustans, or partially independent native states. It is, of course, apartheid's cornerstone that the black man will never be allowed political rights in the white man's territory. To this Dr. Verwoerd added the qualifying clause—"but he can enjoy them to the fullest extent in his own areas." His proposals were put forward in the Promotion of Bantu Self-Government Bill in 1959. This bill proposed the gradual establishment of a number of main "homelands" in which the Bantu would be accorded political rights by degrees and under white control.

"For the first time in their history," declared a White Paper explaining the 1959 law, "the Bantu realize that the European is prepared to grant them full freedom of progress within their own sphere of life. . . ." The key phrase is "within their own sphere." Henceforth the Bantu would have his rights—but only in those territories assigned to him. He could therefore not expect to enjoy them, now or ever, in the territories that the whites had reserved for themselves.

The first of these Bantustans—the 16,000-square-mile Transkei—held its first election in November 1963. The results contradicted Government hopes, "multiracialists" being elected rather than black supporters of apartheid. Precautions had been taken however. The elections involved only a minority—45 of the total seats in the new Transkei Legislative Assembly; the remaining seats—64 of them—were filled by chiefs nominated by the Government, which also paid their salaries. And there were further safeguards, for the law provided that no legislation could be passed by the Transkei Assembly without the agreement of the South African Government, which also

THREE FREE BLACK STATES

Three of the newly independent black states of southern Africa—Lesotho (formerly Basutoland), Swaziland and Botswana (formerly Bechuanaland), occupy lands that are either partly or wholly surrounded by South African territory. Though their peoples share with all the other black Africans the dislike for South Africa's apartheid policies, the climate of hostility is tempered by their economic dependence on the Republic. The largest, Botswana, is arid and thinly populated, but important mineral deposits have been discovered there. Lesotho is a treeless area of eroded soil perched high on the Drakensberg range. Although most of its men work in the mines of South Africa, they proudly reject all suggestions that they join South Africa, because they prefer their political independence. The richest of these three states is Swaziland, which has fertile soil and mineral wealth.

approved all appointments of chiefs or headmen and controlled any colleges or universities that might be set up. At the next election, however, late in 1968, a Government appointee, Chief Matanzima—who had been chosen as Prime Minister following the 1963 election—obtained a majority of the popular votes, having meantime increased his standing among Transkeians by facing up to the Government on several issues and by talking in the terms of African nationalism. But this majority vote would seem to have been cast in favor of getting the utmost out of the existing system, rather than in favor of apartheid as such.

Criticism of the Bantustan scheme, which has come from many quarters, has concentrated chiefly on three points. First, it is obvious that any system of "self-government" that is subject to so much outside interference is not true self-government. Second, the critics point out that the division of the land between blacks and whites is manifestly unfair. The proposed Bantustans include only 13 per cent of South Africa's territory, although the Africans make up 70 per cent of the population. Moreover, the areas lack harbors, mineral wealth and sufficient fertile land, and so can never become self-supporting. Third, the scheme is hypocritical and unworkable since the whites, dependent on the black man's labor, have no intention of really resettling all Africans in such "homelands" far from the factories and mines where the nation's wealth is produced.

From the Nationalist side there has also come criticism that the Bantustans are giveaways of South African territory and that their establishment will involve "enemies within the country's gates," with consequences no one can foresee.

If the Nationalist Party is Afrikanerdom's fighting front, the body that decides its policy and directs strategy is a secret society known as the Broederbond. Formed toward the end of World War I, it originally claimed cultural aspirations, but its driving force was always political ambition. "For Afrikanerdom to reach its ultimate goal of dominance in South Africa. . . ," ran an early circular, "the Broederbond must rule." Once limited to 3,500 members, the Broederbond in the late 1960s had an estimated 8,000, organized on the Communist style into 350 cells. Within the main body is an inner secret society called the Afrikaner Order. At the head of this group is a council modestly known as the Twelve Apostles—each "apostle" overseeing a separate sphere of activity, such as the press, religion or education—with a "trinity" of three "assessors" at the summit.

The aim of the Broederbond is "a Christian Nationalist Calvinist Afrikaner Republic," with Afrikaners supreme in every field of activity. Broeders are expected to support the candidacy of fellow Broeders not only in politics but also in civil and religious life. Eighty per cent of the Nationalist members of Parliament are Broeders, and so are most—though not all—of the men in the Cabinet. Three recent prime ministers were all members. Several thousand Broeders have been recruited from the ranks of headmasters, school inspectors and professors, through whom the organization largely controls education in at least three of the four provinces.

The only political party that could conceivably defeat the Nationalists under the present electoral system is the United Party. But the chance that the United Party might break the Nationalist hold on South Africa's Government grows fainter every year. To win an election, the United Party would have to carry all English-speaking voters and, in addition, 15 per cent of the Afrikaner vote. Afrikaners, bombarded by the Nationalists with frightening stories of the "black menace" and the need for solidarity, have less and less confidence in the United Party's aims and leaders.

Although the United Party opposes the Nationalists

TROUBLED SOUTH-WEST AFRICA

South-West Africa, an immense territory of 317,887 square miles, is currently under international contention. By the terms of the 1920 League of Nations mandate that entrusted government of the area to South Africa, it was agreed that the black majority was to be educated and its material well-being promoted; instead, South Africa has imposed many of its own apartheid laws on the territory. As a result of this, Ethiopia and Liberia filed suit in 1960 with the International Court of Justice—other protests have been voiced in the United Nations General Assembly—with a view to establishing that apartheid is in violation of the original mandate. In 1966 the court rejected the suit by a majority of one, and South Africa has pressed on to incorporate the territory. A number of South-West Africans have been given long prison sentences for attempted guerrilla activities.

on many issues and is liberal enough to frighten many Afrikaners profoundly, its platform on the color issue would hardly please United States advocates of desegregation. Labeled "Discrimination with Justice," the platform calls for integration in the economic sphere but with continued segregation in all other areas. The African must, the United Party leaders affirm, acquire some political rights "one day," though not until he has passed "a long period of training in the ways of democracy. . . ." In South Africa's ever more tense racial situation—which Nationalist policy simultaneously produces and exploits—it has not been difficult for Nationalist Party propaganda to represent the United Party's racial program as "a threat to Western civilization." In addition, recent events throughout the rest of the African continent have been such as to frighten the white voter and to drive him into the arms of any party that is pledged to uphold his privileged position.

THE truly surprising fact, considering the temper of modern South Africa, is not that the United Party is unable to win elections but that it continues to exist at all. The reason is, of course, that many South Africans cannot stomach the policies or the methods of the Nationalists. If the United Party lacks any real alternative policy on the one issue—race relations—that preoccupies every South African voter, it has nonetheless certain strong points of appeal. The first is that it embodies the respect for the rule of law that distinguishes the English-speaking peoples of the world. Second, since the United Party's ideals are general rather than specific and since it believes in providing a climate of tolerance in which leaders of different peoples might work out solutions on a basis of give-and-take rather than by imposed legislation, it is able to draw followers from every quarter. Third, there are many in South Africa to whom the concentration of more and more power into fewer and fewer hands, with the abolition of controls over its possible abuse, is frighteningly reminiscent of the rise of Nazism.

Being the party of big business, the United Party has no serious problem of finance and spends far more on election campaigns than its opponents are able to do. Precisely because of the nature of its backing, however, the party is one that only comes to life for elections and remains dormant in the intervals between them. To the bulk of its supporters, politics is one among many interests. The thousands of United Party supporters and their wives, who dutifully undertake to staff offices and organize meetings when an election looms, abandon it all thankfully the moment that election day is past. The United Party offers nothing to correspond with the Broederbond; it has no secret society, no inner elite, no master plan for achieving domination.

There were until recently two other established political parties enjoying a legal existence in South Africa—the Progressive and the Liberal Parties. Both were formed in the 1950s, dedicated to policies that would guarantee individual liberties; the Liberals also supported a universal franchise. When the Nationalists made all multiracial parties illegal, the Liberals decided to disband, but the Progressive Party fought on. It has only one representative in Parliament, the courageous and determined Mrs. Helen Suzman, who, although she is able to accomplish little, never flinches from raising her voice in protest against Nationalist policies.

The oldest and the best known of nonwhite political organizations is the African National Congress, which was born in the same year as the Nationalist Party (1912) and was banned—along with virtually all other aboveground nonwhite political activity—in April 1960.

The A.N.C. began as a group of educated men who held meetings, passed resolutions and directed appeals to the white Government. By the early 1940s it had become a political party organized on conventional Western lines. It held an annual conference, elected officials and kept membership lists. At different times its organizers claimed a membership ranging from 20,000 to 100,000; in 1960, when it was banned, it may have had as many as 25,000.

FOR years before the Congress was banned, the Nationalists had followed a policy of systematically persecuting all A.N.C. leaders, every one of whom was at different times arrested, fined, imprisoned and banned, some of them many times over. The notorious "Treason Trials," in which a group of leaders mainly but not entirely African was on trial more or less continuously for four years from 1957 to 1961, was an example of such persecution. The court finally threw out the Government's case, acquitting all of the defendants.

Since these trials, the Government has passed a number of laws that give the police such wide powers of arbitrary arrest that they can imprison men for any length of time, never bringing them to court at all. This is done by holding them on suspicion for successive periods of 180 days, rearresting them at the moment each period ends. Besides persecuting the A.N.C. leaders, the Government followed a policy of outlawing, by special legislation, every method of protest that the A.N.C. sought to employ. These laws remain on the books so that even if the A.N.C. were made legal, its leaders would be unable to take any kind of effective political action without immediately being rearrested. They could not hold meetings, advocate a strike, carry placards through the streets or even sit down in the road in protest. A number of them, under the Government's "banning" system, are completely muzzled. It is illegal for any paper or journal or radio station to report not only anything they may say now, but even anything they have *ever* said at any time in the past.

THE A.N.C.—ill-organized, unwieldly and pitifully lacking in funds—was kept active for nearly 50 years by the devotion of a band of Africans who believed that they were building and preparing for a better future. Despite the continual harassment to which they were subjected, their policy remained consistently moderate, and the party's pronouncements thoughtful and dignified. It stood always for a multiracial society in which whites would enjoy full citizenship in a democratic state.

By far the best-known figure in Congress was the late Chief Albert Luthuli, its last President General, who was killed in a railway accident in 1967 when he was aged, sick and almost blind. Known to all Africans as "Chief," he had in fact been dismissed from the leadership of his small Christian sect in Zululand in 1952 by the Nationalist Government. One of the few nonwhite South Africans who had gained a worldwide reputation, Luthuli was awarded the Nobel Peace Prize in 1961.

The second major African movement, which was an offshoot of the A.N.C., was the Pan-African Congress, now also outlawed. Born of impatience with the go-slow tactics and the moderation of the A.N.C., from which it broke away in 1959, the Pan-African aim was "to make the African people conscious of the fact that they have to win their own liberties. . . ." Disdaining the "trade union" methods of the A.N.C.—"telephones are only good for being tapped and membership lists only help the police to arrest all your supporters"—the P.A.C. planned on using quite different techniques: first contact a number of determined men in a few key places; next choose a grievance that affects the whole people deeply; then, on a signal from the leader, let all go into action together.

The first grievance that was chosen was that of the "pass laws." The P.A.C. leader, Robert Sobukwe, gave the word on a Friday in March 1960. On the following Monday all Africans were to burn their hated passbooks and to present themselves at police stations for arrest. One of the few places where the demonstration brought large numbers of people together was at Sharpeville, where the police killed 70 and wounded another 186 in the notorious Sharpeville shootings. Sobukwe and the other P.A.C. leaders were put on trial—not for failing to carry passes as they expected, but for conspiracy and "incitement." They were given sentences of up to three years in jail. When he had served a term of three years, Sobukwe was immediately rearrested and imprisoned under the special police powers.

TODAY those powers have been still further strengthened. One result is that the whole African leadership is scattered. Part of it rots in prison in South Africa. Part of it is dead. Part has escaped —to Tanzania, Ghana, London—there to live the unreal life of exiles who have no idea when, or if, they will ever return to their own country. No new leaders can under the present circumstances emerge, since an African cannot even address a street-corner meeting without being arrested.

And the followers of those leaders, the great mass of more than 13 million black South Africans, remain silent in subjection. But it would be a mistake to suppose that because they have been made politically powerless, they have been deprived of all hope and of every possibility of action.

UNFLINCHING OPPONENT of apartheid, Mrs. Helen Suzman *(right, center)*, lone Progressive Party Member of Parliament, talks politics with a mixed group of students in her Johannesburg living room.

Proud Protest and Tragic Violence

The Nationalist Party rules South Africa with an iron grip. Its principal organized opposition, the United Party, has little hope, as things now stand, of ever again gaining a parliamentary majority. The Nationalists use their power to pass laws making it increasingly hard for the Africans, or any other critics of their racist policies, to organize. Despite all this, a number of opponents have remained determined and vocal. Several English-language newspapers keep up a drumfire of outspoken articles and editorials. Students, writers, churchmen and plain citizens have thrown themselves into efforts to preserve justice. The Africans themselves are voiceless, since their leaders have been imprisoned or forced into exile. Though they are there in millions, they seem powerless to protest against the injustice of their plight.

STUDENT DEMONSTRATORS march through Johannesburg *(below)* to protest the detention without trial of African leaders in 1960. The students were halted by the police, and six of them were arrested.

INNOCENT OR GUILTY?
THE COURTS
NOT THE CABINET
MUST DECIDE.

DEDICATED WOMEN of the Black Sash society *(left)*, including Mrs. Jean Sinclair, the society's head *(center)*, picket against Government policies. Black Sash women sometimes make "vigils" lasting weeks.

OPPOSITION LEADER, Sir de Villiers Graaff *(right)* heads the United Party, which has been notoriously ineffective in preventing the Nationalists from driving their racist programs through Parliament.

SHARPEVILLE, a massacre occurring in 1960, remains a blot on the nation's history

THE SHOOTING BEGINS and the crowd starts to flee *(right)*, some laughing because they think the police are firing blanks. They had gathered in Sharpeville on March 21, 1960, as part of a nationwide protest against the "pass laws." The shooting was touched off when a scuffle followed the arrest of several protest leaders.

FLEEING IN EARNEST, the Africans realize the police are using real ammunition. Two panicky policemen had fired first, without orders, and about 50 others had then opened up, shooting directly into the assembled crowd.

AFTER THE MASSACRE, policemen survey the bodies of the dead and wounded *(right)*. Most had been shot in the back—i.e., while fleeing. Since Sharpeville, laws have been passed forbidding all African demonstrations.

AFRICAN LEADERS have been either imprisoned or officially silenced, although they have generally counseled moderation

ROBERT SOBUKWE, a onetime schoolteacher, spent years in a maximum-security prison for his activities. He was first jailed in 1960 after his party, the now banned Pan-African Congress, had organized the protest against the pass laws that flared into violence at Sharpeville and at Langa.

IEF ALBERT LUTHULI, banned leader of the outlawed can National Congress, lived under house arrest on a farm : Durban *(opposite)*, where he is shown with his wife, daugh- nd grandson. A Nobel laureate, Luthuli worked for African ts while preaching nonviolence until his death in 1967.

NELSON MANDELA, former official of the African National Congress, went on trial for his life in Pretoria in 1963 for allegedly plotting to overthrow the Government. Mandela helped organize underground units to carry on the fight for African rights when his party and Sobukwe's were outlawed in 1960.

WALTER SISULU, like Nelson Mandela, was named a defendant in the "Rivonia trial," so called because the two men, and others on trial, were arrested in the town of Rivonia for plotting sabotage. Both Sisulu *(below)* and Mandela, and all the other defendants save one, were sentenced to life imprisonment in 1964.

OPPOSITION LEADER Knowledge Guzana *(standing)*, head of the Transkei's Democratic Party, addresses the Legislative Assembly. Guzana, who succeeded Chief Victor Poto *(left)*, favors self-government but not independence for black South Africans.

VICTORIOUS CANDIDATE for Transkei Chief Minister, Chief Kaiser Matanzima nominally supports apartheid. He enjoys the backing of the South African Government. But it is often said that inside him a black Nationalist is waiting to get out.

SHOWING THEIR PASSBOOKS, African voters register for the Transkei election. The Transkei, first of the "Bantustans" which has been set aside for the Africans, is partially self-governing, but foreign and other essential policies are controlled by whites.

WAITING TO VOTE, Transkei women dressed in the garb of the Xhosa tribe *(opposite)* gather outside a polling station. More than two thirds of the Transkei electorate voted, despite Government restrictions on political rallies and meetings.

PARTIAL SELF-RULE is exercised by African voters in the Transkei elections

OLD MUTUAL

STREET GAMES in Cape Town's Malay Quarter, a district inhabited by Asians and people of mixed racial descent, entertain a band of children and spectators. In the distance rise the modern office buildings of the city's large business center.

10

New Challenges to the Fortress

UNTIL a very few years ago most white South Africans thought of their country as a beleaguered fortress. It was menaced by the *swart gevaar*—the danger from black Africa; menaced by the rising tide of liberal opinion throughout the world; menaced by a possible uprising of its own voteless black masses. These threats dictated government policy in virtually every field. They were used to justify the stringencies of apartheid, the steady whittling away of the rights even of white citizens to organize and express themselves freely, the ever-growing power of the police, the increasing control over the law courts and the press, and an ever-rising expenditure on arms—which soared from a modest $380,000 in 1960-1961 to $303,600,000 for 1968-1969. They inspired the establishment of a $120,000,000 armaments industry, the construction of a network of strategic roads and airfields over the northern Transvaal, the costly search for self-sufficiency in oil—in short, a determined drive to make the fortress secure and as independent as possible of the outside world.

Events in that outside world have tended since World War II to convince Afrikaner Nationalists of the rightness of their basic policies and of the need to intensify fortress-building efforts. They have also served to enhance enormously the value of their country's assets. Conflict between East and West increased the importance to the Western world of South Africa's mineral wealth; gold has shone out to both people and governments everywhere as the one steady value amid financial, social and political confusion. The 1967 six-day war in the Middle East, closing the Suez Canal, changed shipping routes around Africa, bringing new trade to South African ports and reviving strategic interest in the naval base at Simonstown. Troubles in the black states of Africa were hailed as proof that the black man was generations away from self-government. Race difficulties in the United States, Britain and elsewhere were taken as proof that South Africa's apartheid is the only answer to color enmity.

In the early 1960s almost the only serious debate among Nationalist Afrikaners was between those who argued that the fortress could be held—"at least for my lifetime and my son's"—and those who pessimistically considered that a massive partition of the country would have to be faced. The greater part of South Africa might one day have to be handed over to the blacks, the pessimists thought, but the whites should be able, by planning in time, to secure a retreat for themselves into the western Cape. There they could still enjoy, in the words of Dr. Verwoerd, "white supremacy with poverty in our own laager."

Yet, at the end of the 1960s, only a few years later, there was little talk of retreat to a besieged laager. On the contrary, South African policy had become outward-looking as never before, and the fortress had been transformed from a stronghold for defense into a base for aggressive expansion. The aim—widely accepted though not officially admitted—was to achieve the consolidation of all southern Africa, up to and possibly including the Congo, with its stability guaranteed by the resources—and the forces—of a white South Africa. What had caused this shift in attitude?

THE main causes were two. First, white Rhodesia's declaration of independence; second, the revolutionary movements for independence and freedom among Africans in the Portuguese-held territories of Angola and Mozambique. All three countries had frontiers with South Africa or with South-West Africa, so that changes in their governments were of immediate concern. On November 11, 1965, when the white-supremacist government of Ian Smith declared independence for Rhodesia, the outward reaction in South Africa was one of apprehension over world reaction. But a series of practical steps were quickly taken to mitigate the effect of United Nations sanctions, shore up the Rhodesian economy, and help a friendly neighbor. These included financial aid; the supplying of oil, machinery and military assistance; and a broad extension of trade to offset the loss of other markets. Police collaboration had already been built up over the years. First police and later troops were sent up from South Africa to take part in hunting down guerrillas, particularly in the Zambezi valley. An important aspect of these measures was that they were taken with the full agreement and often with the active cooperation of the Portuguese authorities in Mozambique and Angola. This resulted in the creation of what was in effect an economic and military alliance of the white-governed states of southern Africa. The economic alliance found expression in such projects as the $86 million Cunene River scheme on the border between South-West Africa and Angola, and the $240 million Cabora-Bassa hydroelectric development on the Zambezi River in Mozambique. The military cooperation was exemplified not merely by police and air support sent from South Africa to the Portuguese in Mozambique and Angola but by regular monthly meetings of top-ranking South African, Rhodesian and Portuguese officers in the so-called "Council of Three."

WHERE would all this end? As regards Rhodesia, the growing conviction among Nationalists was that they would find some kind of colony, a sixth province of South Africa, on their hands. Since more than half the white Rhodesians were South Africans by birth or descent, this would be unenthusiastically accepted; it would not ease South Africa's own racial problem if the country acquired some 200,000 whites who brought with them more than four million disaffected Africans. Of greater interest were growing ties with Angola and Mozambique. These colonies had more than 400,000 whites, and this number was expected to grow to one million. In addition, Angola's oil deposits might make southern Africa self-sufficient in this resource. South Africa's horizon, bounded until recently by the Limpopo River, was extended to include some two million square miles of southern Africa, in which 30 million Africans would be under the control of four million whites, with South Africa itself as the arsenal, powerhouse and directing center.

As there were racial and strategic dangers in building close ties with Rhodesia, so there were dangers in involving South Africa's economy and defense too closely with Portuguese-held territories. One danger arose from a difference in policy: the Portuguese were integrationists, not segregationists. A bigger danger was Portugal's home government; Antonio Salazar's dictatorship was fading out, and a future government might be as anxious to reduce Portugal's African commitments as the Salazar regime had been to extend them.

MEANWHILE, alliance with white-controlled territories was hedged by an ambivalent policy towards black independent states. Friendly approaches were mixed with outright threats. Dr. Hastings Banda in Malawi was assisted with construction of his new capital. A black diplomat from Malawi was accepted in Cape Town, and the President of Botswana, Sir Seretse Khama, was welcomed for treatment at a white hospital in Johannesburg. There was cooperation with the newly independent states of Botswana, Lesotho and Swaziland. Confidential trade emissaries were exchanged with Kenya despite the official severance of trade relations. Efforts were made to woo the Malagasy Republic, formerly Madagascar, gaining a toehold in the former French colonies. A harsher tone was used towards Zambia, from which African guerrillas had been entering Rhodesia, and which Vorster threatened in October 1967 to "hit so hard you will never forget it." Yet there was probably no country South Africa wanted more as a friend than Zambia, with its wealth in copper and its "heartland" position on the great continent.

How were these policies received in South Africa itself? There was no doubt that, to the leaders of Afrikaner Nationalism, an expansionist policy appealed partly because it could unite the bulk of white South Africans. It appealed to the English-speaking section because it appeared to break through the narrowness of the old apartheid. It opened up enormous possibilities for the expansion of trade and industry, an aim close to the interests of the English-speaking population. It also promised to mollify the hostility of the outside world by presenting South Africa as a country at once prepared to cooperate in the economic development of black states, and at the same time in a much better position to make such cooperation effective than America or the old colonial powers. But while appealing to the English-speaking, these policies went very much against the grain for many Afrikaners. The danger that has haunted Afrikaners since the time of the Great Trek—a subdivision of the faithful with one group fighting another—had again raised its head.

The division today is into the *verligtes* (the enlightened) and the *verkramptes* (the cramped, or narrow in outlook). Both may for the present be minority groups within the main body of Afrikaner Nationalism, but since they represent two distinct attitudes that must inevitably be expressed through different courses of action, they cannot finally be harmonized without a showdown.

The *verligtes* are comparatively sensitive to world opinion. They believe the Afrikaner can no longer protect himself by being exclusive. South Africa has to evolve a policy that can be sold not only to the world but also to the African continent. This means that it must finally be acceptable also *to the Africans within South Africa.* Basic to this attitude is a new confidence of the Afrikaner in himself, derived from the astonishing growth of his country's prosperity and from the ability of leading Afrikaner businessmen, financiers and scientists to hold their own in the intensity of international competition. The *verligtes* believe that despite ideological differences South Africa can offer more practical assistance to the independent black African states than can any other power, and that by making such help available freely, they will modify and finally dissolve the climate of world hostility.

THE *verkramptes* claim that the traditional policy of building up strength within the laager and of refusing the slightest concession to opponents has been successful almost beyond hope, and that this is no time for change. At home the *verligtes* favor extensive immigration; rapid development of the Bantustans; friendlier attitudes towards the Coloreds, whose leading citizens have been emigrating in numbers; and much more open discussion and debate. The *verkramptes* believe in a minimum of change or open discussion that might lead to change. They maintain that the Afrikaner should cling to his own race, his own language and his own religion; involve himself as little as possible with the ideas of other groups; and insure his survival in his own homeland rather than let himself be drawn into the troubles of a divided continent. Vorster, who became Prime Minister in 1966, is not considered *verligte,* but he dismissed an extreme *verkrampte* Cabinet Minister, Dr. Albert Hertzog, and he backed the *verligtes* on several issues.

To the black majority in South Africa little of all this has yet seeped down either as subject for debate or in the form of any kind of concession. Over the last decade or so the black man's few political liberties and his power to express his views on issues that affect him have been curtailed yet further. He is now not only voteless, but voiceless. Recently, when it would seem that he had no rights left to take away, a ban was imposed on meetings of more than ten people in African areas without special permission—sports and religious gatherings only being excepted.

THE sole improvement in the condition of the nonwhite has been an economic one. The long-continued boom and South Africa's desperate need for skilled and semiskilled labor have allowed many black Africans to get better-paid jobs previously set aside by "job reservation" for "poor whites." In defense plants; in the clothing, laundry, furniture, dry cleaning and textile industries, many thousands of Africans have in effect crossed the color bar to earn pay comparable to that of whites. Many thousands more have been recruited into provincial administration or to do "white man's work" (such as switch operating) on the railways. Among the 250,000 workers engaged in the steel and metal industries, job reservation has virtually dissolved away. The black man, unofficially or under some form of temporary exemption, is doing work from which he is theoretically excluded by apartheid regulations. Even African women have benefited by the change, finding jobs in department stores, shops and factories to replace whites who can earn more as supervisors. In 1958 black Africans attempted a general strike to support a demand for a wage rate of "A Pound a Day," but it failed. Today such rates are not uncommon, and the average number of wage earners per African family in the large location complex of Soweto is said to have risen from 1.3 in 1956 to 2.2 in 1969. Government propaganda claims a growing African "middle class" of some 60,000 families and assumes this means growing contentment of the black man with his lot. It may eventually prove to be so. But the evidence of history tends to show that modest economic improvements do not lead to contentment but to its opposite; revolutions seem to be made by the "contented" middle class, much more than by those who are involved in a desperate struggle to obtain the bare necessities of life.

To sum up: South African Nationalists pay slight regard to the efforts of the outside world to pressure them into changing their apartheid policies. The United States and Britain have far too many troubles of their own to move against South Africa; besides, these powers desperately need both South Africa's gold and the country's availability as a market, since between them they supply nearly 40 per cent of South African imports.

The Nationalists are convinced their fortress is impregnable. The lack of oil was formerly a problem. Now, with possibly two years' supply in storage, an unlimited flow from the Middle East and discoveries in Angola, this causes less anxiety. South-West Africa was called the Achilles' heel because its indeterminate status suggested that it might become a base of rebellion against the South African government. The International Court of Justice removed that danger by endorsing South Africa's claim to rule the territory. The combination of powerful military presence there with the establishment of a Bantustan for the region's 300,000 Ovambos should take care of the future. South African Nationalism has never been riding higher than it is today.

BUT in a strange way, while the battles are being won, control over the war is being lost. In the interests of an expansionist policy and under the pressures of great economic growth, modifications of apartheid policy have had to be accepted. It will be ironic if self-interest eventually causes changes that have been bitterly opposed on ideological and religious grounds. But would such a result be any stranger than that the dream of Cecil Rhodes—arch-fiend in Afrikaner mythology—for a white-dominated southern half of Africa should have been taken over by Afrikaners as basis for the new "enlightenment"?

African miners look on as a fellow worker at the Eastern Rand Proprietary Mines near Johannesburg learns to operate a hoist.

A BOOMING ECONOMY'S *need for labor challenges restrictive policies . . .*

A white policeman halts an apprehensive African in Sophiatown, a Johannesburg suburb, on the day in 1955 when Africans were

. . . as more black Africans are admitted to jobs of higher pay and status in the face

evicted and moved to a new township. The African families, whose homes were later razed, were not permitted a voice in the matter.

of Afrikaners' inflexible determination to preserve white privilege and domination

Appendix

HISTORICAL DATES

1488 Portuguese navigator Bartholemew Dias discovers the Cape of Good Hope

1652 Jan van Riebeeck establishes the first settlement at the Cape

1657 Slaves first imported from Java, Madagascar and West Africa

1688 Arrival of French Huguenots

1779 The first "Kaffir Wars" between Europeans and African tribes

1795-1803 First British occupation of the Cape

1803-1806 Control of the Cape is returned to the Dutch settlers. The British again assume control

1820 Arrival of 5,000 British immigrants

1834 Slavery is abolished in the Cape

1836 Great Trek from the Cape begins

1838 Massacre of Boers by the Zulu chief Dingaan. Andries Pretorius defeats Dingaan. Republic of Natal is founded

1843 Natal is annexed by the British Government

1852-1854 Britain formally recognizes independence of Transvaal and Orange Free State

1867 Diamonds are discovered

1886 Gold is discovered on the Witwatersrand

1890 Cecil Rhodes becomes Prime Minister of the Cape

1899-1902 Boer War followed by the Treaty of Vereeniging. Orange Free State and Transvaal are made British colonies

1902 Death of Cecil Rhodes

1904 Chinese are imported to work in the gold mines. Paul Kruger dies

1910 The Act of Union is passed by the British Parliament. Louis Botha is the first Prime Minister of a unified South Africa

1910-1924 African Reserves are set aside and the rights of Africans to acquire land elsewhere is curtailed. First Natives (Urban Areas) Act is passed limiting the numbers of, and segregating, Africans in the cities. The first legal color bar concerning employment in the mines and public works is adopted

1912 The African National Congress (A.N.C.) is formed to fight for the rights of Africans

1913 Nationalist Party founded by J.B.M. Hertzog

1914-1918 South Africa enters World War I

1919 South Africa is granted a mandate over South-West Africa by League of Nations. General Botha dies and General Smuts becomes Prime Minister

1924 Hertzog becomes Prime Minister

1924-1933 A "civilized" policy for labor is adopted reserving certain jobs for whites and establishing a higher wage scale for them

1927 Extramarital intercourse between whites and Africans becomes a criminal offense

1931 Statute of Westminster is passed by Britain's Parliament, giving South Africa full freedom to pass its own legislation

1933 A coalition of Nationalist and South African Parties wins control of the Government. The United Party is formed

1936 African voters in the Cape are removed from the common roll

1937 The rights of Africans to acquire land outside their Reserves is further curtailed; the influx of Africans to the towns is even more tightly limited. Strikes by African workers become illegal

1939-1945 South African forces fight in World War II

1948 The Nationalist Party wins power with Dr. D. F. Malan as Prime Minister

1948-1953 Apartheid is defined through legislation. The Government is enabled to ban organizations, publications and persons suspected of "Communism"; the population is divided into racial categories; the voting rights of Indians, Coloreds and Africans are diminished or withdrawn and a new form of local government for Africans in the Reserves is created

1951-1953 Indians and Africans join to defy Government policies

1953-1955 Most primary and secondary education is taken over by the Government

1954 Dr. Malan retires; J. G. Strijdom becomes Prime Minister

1956-1960 The "pass laws" are tightened, causing numerous demonstrations including bus boycotts

1958 The four-year Treason Trial begins: all defendants are acquitted in 1961. J. G. Strijdom dies and Dr. H. F. Verwoerd is chosen as Prime Minister

1959 Robert Sobukwe is elected president of the Pan-African Congress (P.A.C.), an activist offshoot of the African National Congress. An act is passed abolishing the Parliamentary representation of Africans

1959-1963 The Transkei becomes a separate territory and acquires limited self-government. Africans are allowed to live outside their "homelands" only while working for whites in capacities determinable by the Government

1960 In most of the large cities Africans, led by Sobukwe's P.A.C., demonstrate against the pass laws. At Sharpeville this leads to the massacre of 70 Africans

1961 Dr. Verwoerd attends the Commonwealth Conference in London and applies for continued membership, but he withdraws his application when South Africa's racial policies are severely criticized by other heads of state. On May 31, South Africa becomes a republic

1962 The United Nations General Assembly votes in favor of diplomatic and economic sanctions against South Africa. The Group Areas Act is amended to reinforce the physical separation of the races

1963 The police are empowered to arrest without warrant—and to detain without trial—anyone suspected of a political offense

1964 Several important African nationalist leaders are sentenced to life imprisonment for political activities

1965 Declaration of independence by Rhodesia under Ian Smith

1966 Assassination of Dr. Verwoerd. B. J. Vorster becomes Prime Minister. The charges against South Africa in the International Court of Justice repeated. Termination by the United Nations of the South-West Africa mandates. Botswana and Lesotho become independent

1967 South Africa sends armed police to aid Rhodesian whites against African guerrillas

1968 First black diplomat from an independent state (Malawi) accepted in South Africa. Introduction of two-ties system for gold prices with international pressure in South Africa to sell gold on the free market. Swaziland becomes independent

FOR FURTHER READING

CHAPTER 1: THE LAND AND ITS PEOPLE

Cowles, Raymond B., *Zulu Journal, Field Notes of a Naturalist in South Africa.* University of California Press, 1959.

Marquard, Leo, *The Peoples & Policies of South Africa.* Oxford University Press, 1962.

Millin, Sarah Gertrude, *The People of South Africa.* Alfred A. Knopf, 1954.

Morris, James, *South African Winter.* Pantheon, 1958.

Paton, Alan, *The Land and People of South Africa.* Lippincott, 1955.

Segal, Ronald, *Into Exile.* McGraw-Hill, 1963.

Van den Berghe, Pierre L., *South Africa, A Study in Conflict.* Wesleyan University Press, 1965.

Walker, Eric A., gen'l. ed., *The Cambridge History of the British Empire,* Volume VIII, *South Africa.* Cambridge University Press, 1963.

Wellington, J. H., *Southern Africa.* Cambridge University Press, 1955.

CHAPTER 2: SETTLING THE LAND

De Kiewiet, C. W., *A History of South Africa, Social & Economic.* Oxford University Press, 1960.

Fage, J. D., *An Atlas of African History.* Edward Arnold, London, 1961.

Geen, M. S., *The Making of the Union of South Africa.* Longmans, Green and Co., 1947.

Hofmeyr, Jan H., *South Africa.* 2nd rev. ed. by J. P. Cope, McGraw-Hill, 1952.

Keppel-Jones, Arthur, *South Africa, A Short History.* Hutchinson & Co., London, 1963.

Marquard, Leo, *The Story of South Africa.* Roy Publishers, 1955.

Oliver, Roland, and J. D. Fage, *A Short Short History of Africa.* Penguin Books, 1963.

Walker, Eric A., *A History of Southern Africa.* Longmans, Green and Co., 1957.

CHAPTER 3: THE CHANGING ECONOMY

Davidson, Basil, *Report on Southern Africa.* Jonathan Cape, London, 1952.

Houghton, D. Hobart, *The South African Economy.* Oxford University Press, 1964.

Hurwitz, N., and O. Williams, *The Economic Framework of South Africa.* Shuter, Shuter & Shooter, Pietermaritzburg, 1962.

Jeppe, C. B., *Gold Mining on the Witwatersrand.* Transvaal Chamber of Mines, Johannesburg, 1946.

Lewinsohn, Richard, *Barney Barnato.* E. P. Dutton, 1938.

Lockhart, J. G., and C. M. Woodhouse, *Cecil Rhodes, the Colossus of Southern Africa.* The Macmillan Co., 1963.

South African Prospects and Progress, Information Service of South Africa, New York, 1963.

CHAPTER 4: THE BOER WAR

Gross, Felix, *Rhodes of Africa.* Frederick A. Praeger, 1957.

Hancock, W. K., *Smuts: The Sanguine Years 1870-1919.* Cambridge University Press, 1962.

Holt, Edgar, *The Boer War.* Putnam, London, 1958.

Kruger, Rayne, *Good-Bye Dolly Gray, The Story of the Boer War.* Lippincott, 1960.

Marais, J. S., *The Fall of Kruger's Republic.* Oxford University Press, 1961.

Smuts, J. C., *Jan Christian Smuts.* Morrow, 1952.

Thompson, Leonard M., *The Unification of South Africa 1902-1910.* Oxford University Press, 1960.

CHAPTER 5: THE LIFE OF THE WHITES

Calpin, G. H., ed., *The South African Way of Life: Values and Ideals of a Multi-racial Society.* Columbia University Press, 1953.

De Beer, Z. J., *Multi-racial South Africa.* Oxford University Press, 1961.

Patterson, Sheila, *The Last Trek, A Study of the Boer People and the Afrikaner Nation.* Routledge & Kegan Paul, London, 1957.

Spooner, F. P., *South African Predicament, The Economics of Apartheid.* Frederick A. Praeger, 1961.

Van Jaarsveld, F. A., *The Awakening of Afrikaner Nationalism.* Human & Rousseau, Cape Town, 1961.

CHAPTER 6: AFRICANS AND APARTHEID

Doxey, G. V., *The Industrial Colour Bar in South Africa.* Oxford University Press, 1961.

Hopkinson, Tom, *In the Fiery Continent.* Doubleday, 1963.

Horrell, Muriel, *A Survey of Race Relations in South Africa.* (Annual) South African Institute of Race Relations, Johannesburg. *Race Relations Journal.* (Quarterly) South African Institute of Race Relations, Johannesburg.

Jabavu, Noni, *Drawn in Color.* St Martin's Press, 1962.

Jabavu, Noni, *The Ochre People, Scenes from a South African Life.* St Martin's Press, 1963.

Mphahlele, Ezekiel, *Down Second Avenue.* Faber and Faber, London, 1959.

Neame, L. E., *The History of Apartheid.* London House & Maxwell, 1963.

Patterson, Sheila, *Colour and Culture in South Africa.* Routledge & Kegan Paul, London, 1953.

Richmond, A., *The Colour Problem.* Penguin Books, 1961.

Sampson, Anthony, *Drum, A Venture into the New Africa.* Collins, London, 1956.

Wilson, Monica, and Archie Mafeje, *Langa, A Study of Social Groups in an African Township.* Oxford University Press, 1963.

CHAPTER 7: RELIGION

Carter, Gwendolen M., *The Politics of Inequality.* Frederick A. Praeger, 1959.

Grant, Edward W., *South Africa: What of the Church?* Edinburgh House Press, 1952.

Huddleston, Trevor, C. R., *Naught for Your Comfort.* Doubleday, 1956.

Munger, Edwin S., *Christians and Race Relations in South Africa* (Parts I & II). American Universities Field Staff, 1961.

Reeves, Ambrose, *South Africa—Yesterday and Tomorrow.* Victor Gollancz, London, 1962.

Visser't Hooft, Dr. Willem Adolph, *Christianity, Race and the South African People.* National Council of the Churches of Christ in the U.S.A., 1952.

CHAPTER 8: THE ARTS

Alexander, F. L., *Art in South Africa, Painting, Sculpture and Graphic Work since 1900.* A. A. Balkema, Cape Town, 1962.

Butler, Guy, *A Book of South African Verse.* Oxford University Press, 1963.

Gordon-Brown, A., *Pictorial Art in South Africa, During Three Centuries to 1875.* Chas. J. Sawyer, London, 1952.

Grove, A. P., and C.J.D. Harvey, eds., *Afrikaans Poems with English Translations.* Oxford University Press, 1963.

Hughes, Langston, ed., *An African Treasury.* Crown Publishers, 1960.

McLeod, A. L., ed., *The Commonwealth Pen*. Cornell University Press, 1961.

Malcolm, D. McK., and Florence L. Friedman, *Zulu Horizons, The Vilakazi Poems Rendered into English*. Bailey Bros. & Swinfen, London, 1962.

Mphahlele, Ezekiel, *The African Image*. Faber & Faber, London, 1962.

Rutherfoord, Peggy, ed., *African Voices, An Anthology of Native African Writing*. The University Library, Grosset & Dunlap, 1960.

The South African Tradition. Information Service of South Africa, New York, 1963.

CHAPTER 9: MODERN POLITICS

Benson, Mary, *The African Patriots*. Faber and Faber, London, 1963.

Carter, Gwendolen M., *The Politics of Inequality*. Frederick A. Praeger, 1959.

Krüger, D. W., *South African Parties and Policies 1910-1960*. Human & Rousseau, Cape Town, 1960.

Lewin, Julius, *Politics and Law in South Africa*. Merlin Press, London, 1963.

Reeves, Ambrose, *Shooting at Sharpeville*. Houghton Mifflin, 1961.

Segal, Ronald, *Political Africa, A Who's Who of Personalities and Parties*. Frederick A. Praeger, 1961.

CHAPTER 10: PRESENT AND FUTURE

Calvocoressi, Peter, *South Africa and World Opinion*. Oxford University Press, 1961.

Luthuli, Albert, *Let My People Go*. McGraw-Hill, 1962.

Ngubane, Jordan K., *An African Explains Apartheid*. Frederick A. Praeger, 1963.

Paton, Alan, *Hope for South Africa*. Frederick A. Praeger, 1959.

Pienaar, S., and Anthony Sampson, *Two Views of Separate Development*. Oxford University Press, 1960.

Sampson, Anthony, *Common Sense about Africa*. The Macmillan Co., 1962.

SOUTH AFRICAN CULTURAL FIGURES AND THEIR PRINCIPAL WORKS

PAINTING AND SCULPTURE		
Bowler, Thomas W.	1813-1869	London-taught painter who did many watercolors of South Africa
Baines, Thomas	1820-1875	Most prolific 19th Century painter, who recorded the South African scene in detail
Volschenk, Jan Ernst Abraham	1853-1936	Called the first Afrikaner artist. A romantic realist, he painted meticulous and photographic landscapes
Naudé, Hugo	1869-1941	Landscape and portrait painter. Studied in London, later adjusted palette to South Africa's sunny climate and bright scenery
Goodman, Gwelo	1871-1939	Still lifes, interiors, landscapes and architectural subjects
Kottler, Moses	1896-	Sculptor noted for public monuments and massive figures. Works in bronze, wood and stone
Welz, Jean	1897 (?)-	Painter of figures, landscapes, portraits, still lifes, and abstract nonfigurative compositions
Coetzer, Willem Hermanus	1900-	Realistic painter of still lifes, landscapes, seascapes and historical events. Designed marble frieze for Voortrekker monument
Lipshitz, Lippy	1903-	Sculptor born in Russia: *The Tree of Life, Jacob Wrestling with Angel*
Steynberg, Coert	1905-	Monuments and equestrian statues. Also figures in metal for public buildings: *Our Hope, The Glanstoring*
Battiss, Walter	1906-	Authority on Bushman cave paintings. A teacher as well as painter, he has written several books on prehistoric art
Higgs, Cecil	1906-	Abstract compositions of sea forms. Charcoal drawings and mixed medium
Boonzaier, Gregoire	1909-	Watercolorist of still lifes and simple everyday scenes. Won Medal of Honour of Die Suid-Afrikaanse Akademie in 1958. Attention to texture and color
Stern, Irma	191?-	Brought German Expressionism to South Africa in her landscapes, paintings of figures and still lifes. Noted for versatility and color sense.
Laubser, Maggie	19??-	Applies doctrines of German Expressionism to South African themes. Awarded Medal of Honour of Die Suid-Afrikaanse Akademie in 1949
Preller, Alexis	1911-	Painter who does both abstract and representational works. He has painted murals for public buildings in Pretoria
Sekoto, Gerard	1913-	Painter who emigrated to Paris. Combines realism and impressionism: *The Proud Father*
Cilliers-Barnard, Bettie	1914-	Abstract painter and graphic artist with a sure sense of design, color and form
Potgieter, Hendrik	1916-	Sculptor of public monuments and statues: *Liberty Curbed*
Villa, Edoardo	1920-	Sculptor, born in Italy. He does abstracts in steel, bronze, plaster and reconstructed stone.
Vorster, Gordon	1924-	Abstract expressionism in oils: *Bird Mountain, Kalahari Kloof*
Sash, Cecily	1925-	Abstract and nonfigurative painter and graphic artist. Also murals and mosaics
Sithole, Lucas	1932-	African sculptor working in wood and metals: *Friendship, The Thinker*
Kumalo, Sidney	1935-	Zulu sculptor who does powerful wooden figures: *St. Francis*
MUSIC		
Fagan, Johannes	1898-1920	Studied in London, wrote first serious South African symphonic work: *Prelude*. Also song, "Die Soekende Moeder"

Fagan, Gideon	1904-	Conductor and composer of concert works, songs and music for motion pictures: *Ilala, Tears*
Gerstman, Blanche	1910-	Vocal works. Cantatas: *Uit die Passie*
Van Wyk, Arnold	1916-	Pianist and composer of symphonic and choral music: His song-cycle *Van Liefde en Verlatenheid* won award at the international festival of music in Israel in 1955
Du Plessis, Hubert	1922-	Composer. Many of his works have been published in London, including vocal works for soloists and chorus as well as piano compositions
Grové, Stefaans	1922-	Pianist and composer. He has worked abroad, lecturing at the Peabody Conservatory in Baltimore, Maryland. His works include *Divertimento* for woodwind and *Symphonie Concertanto*
Joubert, John	1927-	Worked abroad lecturing in music at the University of Hull, England
LITERATURE		
Schreiner, Olive	1855-1920	Novelist: *The Story of an African Farm*
Celliers, Jan F. E.	1865-1940	Poet in Afrikaans: "The Plain," "Kruger"
Marais, Eugène N.	1871-1936	Poet in Afrikaans: "Winter's Night," "Soul of the White Ant"
Lewis, Ethelreda	1875-1946	Editor and writer. Novels: *Trader Horn* books
Plaatje, Solomon T.	1875-1932	Wrote in English and in the Tswana language. Prose: *Mhudi*
Smith, Pauline	18??-1959	Novelist and short-story writer. Novels: *The Beadle, Platkop's Children*
Slater, Francis Carey	1876-1958	Poet and patron of South African writing in English. *Dark Folk, The Karroo, Drought*
Mofolo, Thomas	1877-1948	Prose written in the Sesotho language: historical novel, *Chaka*
Totius (J. D. du Toit)	1877-1953	Poet in Afrikaans: "The Will of God," "The Earth Is Not Our Dwelling Place"
Leipoldt, C. Louis	1880-1947	Poet in Afrikaans: "Peace Night," "The Worst Horror"
Millin, Sarah Gertrude	1889-1968	Novelist: *God's Stepchildren, The Dark River*
Cloete, Stuart	1897-	Novelist. Emigrant from South Africa. *Turning Wheels, Against These Three*
Du Plessis, I. D.	1900-	Poet in Afrikaans: "Katrina"
Campbell, Roy	1901-1957	Outstanding South African poet in English. Poetry: *The Flaming Terrapin, The Wayzgoose, Adamastor*
Van den Heever, C. M.	1902-1957	Poet in Afrikaans: "Birds at Twilight"
Paton, Alan	1903-	Novelist, teacher and principal of a Johannesburg reformatory. *Cry, the Beloved Country, Too Late the Phalarope, Tales from a Troubled Land, South Africa in Transition*
Plomer, William	1903-	Poet, novelist and short-story writer. Novels: *Turbott Wolfe, Museum Pieces.* Stories: *"I Speak of Africa"*
Bosman, Herman Charles	1905-1951	Novelist, poet and journalist. Novels: *Mafeking Road, Cold Stone Jug*
Dhlomo, H.I.E.	1905-1956	Journalist, poet and playwright. Poetry: "The Valley of a Thousand Hills." Plays: *Shaka, Cetewayo*
Sowden, Lewis	1905-	Journalist, playwright and novelist. Prose: *The Crooked Bluegum*
Jordan, A. C.	1906-	Teacher, critic and writer of prose and poetry in both English and the Xhosa language. "The Wrath of the Ancestors"
Van Wyk Louw, N. P.	1906-	Leading poet in Afrikaans: *Raka,* "The Prophet"
Vilakazi, Benedict Wallet	1906-1947	Teacher and outstanding writer of prose and poetry in Zulu: *Zulu Horizons*
Krige, Uys	1910-	Writer of prose and poetry in Afrikaans and English. Prose: *The Way Out*
Bloom, Harry	1913-	Prose: *Episode.* Play: *King Kong*
Louw, W.E.G.	1913-	Afrikaans-speaking poet: *Adam,* "Last Supper," "Quiet Evening"
Opperman, D. J.	1914-	Poet who writes in Afrikaans: "A Letter Home," "Slag-heap Ballad"
Petersen, S. V.	1914-	Poet in Afrikaans: "Conclusion"
Eybers, Elisabeth	1915-	Afrikaans-speaking poet. Emigrant from South Africa. Poetry: "Witwatersrand," "Snail"
Delius, Anthony	1916-	Poet, journalist, playwright, editor, writer of fiction and travel books. Verse: *An Unknown Border.* Fiction: *The Day Natal Took Off*
Butler, Guy	1918-	Professor at Rhodes University, editor of literary journal *Standpunte.* Poetry: *Stranger to Europe.* Plays: *The Dam, The Dove Returns*
Abrahams, Peter	1919-	Prose writer now in exile: *Tell Freedom, Return to Goli, Mine Boy*
Brown, James Ambrose	1919-	Journalist, playwright and novelist. Prose: *Splendid Sunday*
Mphahlele, Ezekiel	1919-	Writer in exile, teacher and critic. Autobiography: *Down Second Avenue.* Critique: *The African Image*
Jabavu, Noni	1920(?)-	Novelist in exile. *Drawn in Color, The Ochre People*
Matshikiza, Todd	1921(?)-1968	Journalist and musician. Composed the score for the musical *King Kong.* Autobiography: *Chocolates for my Wife*
Philander, P. J.	1921-	Poet in Afrikaans: "Winter Evening"
Gordimer, Nadine	1923-	Short stories and novels: *Occasion for Loving, The Soft Voice of the Serpent, The Lying Days*
Macnab, Roy	1923-	Journalist, editor and poet. Prose: *Testament of a South African*
Modisane, Bloke	1923-	Journalist now in exile. Autobiography: *Blame Me on History, Why I Ran Away*
Sentso, Dyke	1924-	Teacher and writer of prose in English and in the Sesotho language: *Under the Blue Gum Trees*
Themba, Can	1924-1968	Journalist and short-story writer: *Requiem for Sophiatown, Mob Passion*
Jacobson, Dan	1929-	Novels and social criticism. Emigrant from South Africa. *A Dance in the Sun*
Kumalo, Peter (Peter Clark)	1929-	Artist and writer. Short stories: *Death in the Sun*
Rive, Richard	1931-	Writer and teacher. Short-story collection: *African Songs*
Fugard, Atholl	1932-	Playwright: *The Blood Knot*

Credits

The sources for the illustrations in this book appear below. Credits for pictures from left to right are separated by commas, from top to bottom by dashes.

Cover—Grey Villet
8—Grey Villet
11—Map by Rafael Palacios
15 through 24—Grey Villet
31—Map by Rafael Palacios
33 through 40—Grey Villet
44—Drawing by David Greenspan
48 through 51—Grey Villet
52—Terence Spencer for FORTUNE
53, 54, 55—Grey Villet
56, 57—Courtesy Radio Times Hulton Picture Library
58, 59—Culver Pictures
61—Map by Rafael Palacios
64 through 67—Courtesy Radio Times Hulton Picture Library
68, 69, 70—Grey Villet
79 through 88—Grey Villet
96 through 107—Grey Villet
112 through 115—Grey Villet
116, 117—Terence Spencer
123 through 126—Grey Villet
127—Michael Peto—Grey Villet
128, 129—Terence Spencer
136, 137—Terence Spencer except bottom right Cloete Breytenback for TIME
138, 139—Ian Berry from Magnum except bottom Warwick Robinson
140—Terence Spencer
141—*Drum* photo, Ernest Shirley—Terence Spencer
142—Grey Villet except top left no credit
143, 144—Grey Villet
149—Grey Villet
150, 151—Alan Peake

ACKNOWLEDGMENTS

The editors wish to express their appreciation to Gwendolen M. Carter, Professor of Political Science and Director of African Studies at Northwestern University, and to Thomas G. Karis, Professor of Political Science at the City College of New York, both of whom commented in detail on the text chapters.

Index

** This symbol in front of a page number indicates a photograph or painting of the subject mentioned.*

xxx

Production staff for Time Incorporated

John L. Hallenbeck (Vice President and Director of Production)

Robert E. Foy and Caroline Ferri

Text photocomposed under the direction of Albert J. Dunn

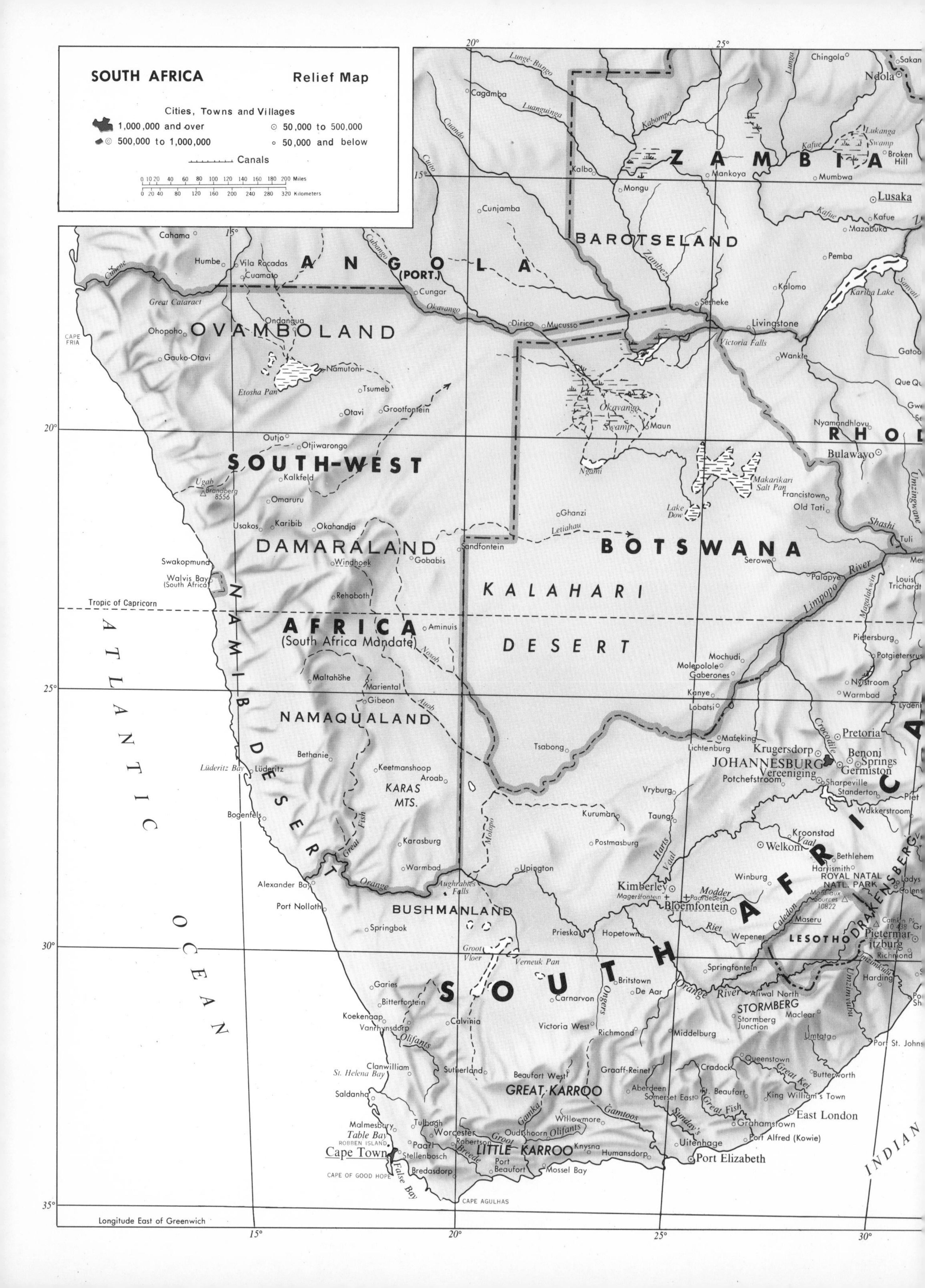

SOUTH AFRICA
Relief Map
Cities, Towns and Villages
1,000,000 and over
500,000 to 1,000,000
50,000 to 500,000
50,000 and below
Canals
Miles
Kilometers
ANGOLA (PORT.)
ZAMBIA
BAROTSELAND
OVAMBOLAND
SOUTH-WEST AFRICA (South Africa Mandate)
DAMARALAND
NAMAQUALAND
NAMIB DESERT
KALAHARI DESERT
BOTSWANA
RHOD
SOUTH AFRICA
BUSHMANLAND
GREAT KARROO
LITTLE KARROO
LESOTHO
DRAKENSBERG
STORMBERG
KARAS MTS.
ATLANTIC OCEAN
INDIAN
Tropic of Capricorn
Longitude East of Greenwich
Etosha Pan
Okavango Swamp
Makarikari Salt Pan
Lake Dow
Ngami
Victoria Falls
Kariba Lake
Lukanga Swamp
Great Cataract
Aughrabies Falls
Groot Vloer
Verneuk Pan
St. Helena Bay
Table Bay
False Bay
ROBBEN ISLAND
CAPE OF GOOD HOPE
CAPE AGULHAS
CAPE FRIA
Lüderitz Bay
Alexander Bay
Walvis Bay (South Africa)
Brandberg 8556
Mont aux Sources 10822
ROYAL NATAL NATL. PARK
Cape Town
JOHANNESBURG
Pretoria
Port Elizabeth
East London
Bloemfontein
Kimberley
Windhoek
Lusaka
Bulawayo
Livingstone
Ndola
Chingola
Broken Hill
Gaberones
Pietermaritzburg